NAVIA was founded in 2004 as a business-college project for the then 22-year-old Óli Kristian á Torkilsheyggi, now the CEO. Navia is a family-run company that continues a long tradition of sheep-rearing and wool-spinning. Óli Kristian's great-grandmother, Suffía Gregersen, employed women to knit for her and sold sweaters in the Faroese village of Syðrugøta, where the family had a spinning mill; and the family's farm had a flock of 200 sheep, so Óli learned about wool at an early age.

The first items produced by Navia were 1-, 2- and 3-ply yarns in six natural colours, and a small amount of plain-coloured sock wool. These were sold to yarn shops, cottage industry associations and even to small supermarkets all over the country.

In the years that followed, Navia grew bigger and produced a wider range of yarns. A new knitting book came out each year, more colours were added to the palette of yarn colours, and the yarn began to be sold overseas.

Since 2004 Navia has grown from a one-man enterprise with only a few different types of yarn to a company exporting yarn worldwide.

www.navia.fo

Instagram: @naviafaroeislands

TRADITIONAL KNITS FROM THE FAROE ISLANDS

TRADITIONAL KNITS FROM THE FAROE ISLANDS

Navia

SEARCH PRESS

Photos

Page 16: Public Domain, Johannes Klein, 1898, National Museum, Denmark.
Page 20: Left © Olivia Thorkilshøj
Page 55: Left © Petra Arge
Page 57: Left © Petra Arge. Right © Dagmar Sjúrðardóttir

Bibliography

Annika Skaalum: *Føroyskt heimavirki – millum fortíð og framtíð* [*Faroese home-work – between the past and the future*], 2006 (Master's thesis)

Framsýning á Tjóðsavninum um seyð og ull [Exhibition at the National Museum of Sheep and Wool], Spring 2023

Um ull og tøting – samrøða hjá Niels Juel Arge við Suffíu Gregersen í 1957 ['About wool and knitting' – interview by Niels Juel Arge with Suffíu Gregersen in 1957], 4 September 2020 (KVF – Faroe Islands broadcasting company)

Robert Joensen: *Seyðabókin* [*The Sheep Book*], Sprotin, 2015 (re-issue)

Olav Schneider: *Seyður og seyðahald, Bókadeild Føroya Lærarafelags* [*Sheep and Sheep Farming*, Book Department of the Faroese Teachers' Association], 2015

Hans Marius Debes: *Føroysk Bindingarmynstur* [*Faroese Knitting Patterns*], 1969

www.heimabeiti.fo

TRADITIONAL KNITS FROM THE FAROE ISLANDS

First published in the UK in 2025 by
Search Press Limited
Wellwood, North Farm Road,
Tunbridge Wells, Kent TN2 3DR

Originally published as *Ull*
Copyright © Navia and Bogoo Books, 2023.
English edition published in agreement with Bennet Agency

Knitwear designs and photos © Navia
Design, layout and typesetting: Paula S. á Torkilsheyggi
Text: Óluva Zachariasen
Editing: Julie Pedersen
Knitwear designs: Sára J. Mrdalo, Tóra Joensen,
Gunnvør Frederiksberg, Oddvör Jacobsen, Sigbritt Friis,
Dagmar Beder and Harriet Jørginsdóttir
Photos: Beinta á Torkilsheyggi, Óluva á Torkilsheyggi
and Paula S. á Torkislsheyggi

English translation from the original Danish by
Tankerton Translations

ISBN: 978-1-80092-311-9
ebook ISBN: 978-1-80093-298-2

MIX
Paper | Supporting
responsible forestry
FSC
www.fsc.org
FSC® C016973

Bookmarked Hub

For further ideas and inspiration, and to join our free online
community, visit www.bookmarkedhub.com

Publishers' notes

Metric measurements are used in this book; the imperial
conversions are rounded to the nearest ¼in. Always use either
metric or imperial measurements, not a combination of both.

The Publishers and author can accept no responsibility for
any consequences arising from the information, advice or
instructions given in this publication.

Readers are permitted to reproduce any of the projects in this
book for their personal use, or for the purpose of selling for
charity, free of charge and without the prior permission of the
Publishers. You are not permitted to use any of the projects for
commercial purposes, or for the purpose of training artificial
intelligence technologies or systems.

We do our best to ensure that all of our books are error-free.
If you spot anything that's not quite right, check our website
(www.searchpress.com) or the Bookmarked Hub
(www.bookmarkedhub.com) to find any mistakes we've
already fixed.

You are invited to visit the authors' website: www.navia.fo

GPSR information can be found at www.searchpress.com

The Faroese knitting company Navia is now
20 years old. We are very grateful for the
wonderful support we have received over the years,
both in the Faroes and our neighbouring countries;
your interest and support means everything.
This book is our way of celebrating a milestone
birthday by looking at the history of Navia and
the inspiration for the company. You will meet
some of the people behind Navia and you can
read about Faroese wool, sheep, knitting patterns,
knitting clubs, the way the patterns are created and
the latest knitting techniques. And you will also
find 28 of the best patterns we have published over
the years. We hope that these and reading about
us will inspire you to get knitting and enjoy the
fantastic resource that we have in wool.

Happy knitting!

Óli Kristian and Paula S. á Torkilsheyggi

CONTENTS

THE NAVIA PATTERNS 66

THE FAROE ISLANDS, THE FARM AND THE SHEEP

THE FAROE ISLANDS

The Faroes are a group of 18 small islands located in the middle of the North Atlantic. In winter, the salt spray from the waves hammers at the cliffs; in summer, fairytale green slopes flourish below the steep rocky heights.

At 1,399 square kilometres (870 square miles) and with barely 55,000 inhabitants, the Faroe Islands are one of the world's smallest nations. Along with Greenland, the Faroe Islands are part of the Kingdom of Denmark but have their own parliament, language, culture and flag. The first inhabitants arrived about 1,500 years ago. Genetic research shows that the women and men who originally settled in the Faroes came from different areas: the women originated mainly from Ireland and the British Isles, whereas the men came from Norway.

The Faroese make their living chiefly from fishing, salmon farming and some tourism. The islands have a well-developed IT infrastructure, a good road network with undersea tunnels and a number of restaurants serving everything from sushi to fermented meat and dried fish.

The Faroe islanders own sheep and cars. They drink lattes, dance the Faroese chain dance, listen to the latest music, knit, post photos on Instagram and hold rowing races. There are both vegans and people who eat fulmars and sheep's heads. The Faroes are a complex nation, in which tradition and modernity flourish side by side.

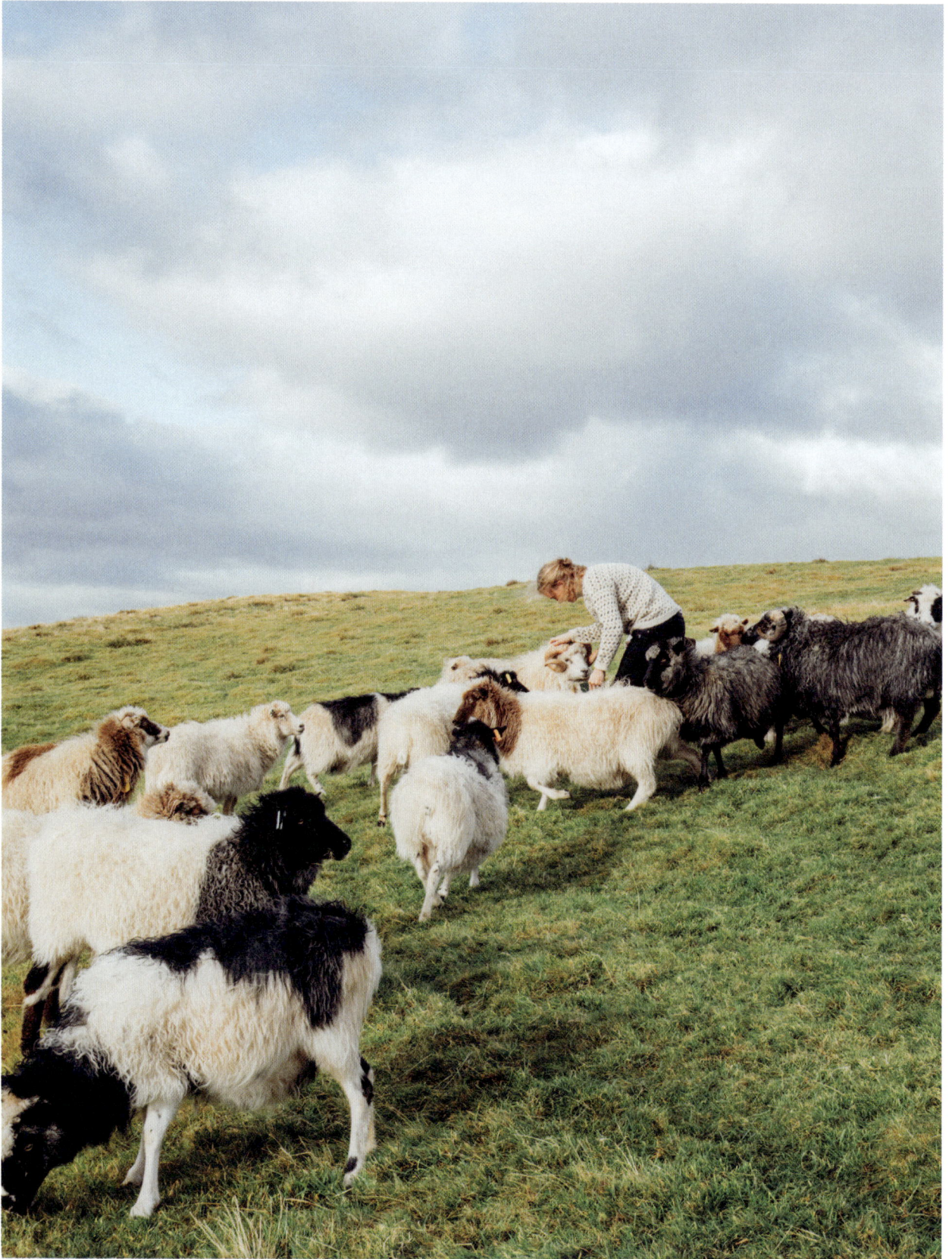

FAROESE SHEEP

There are well over 70,000 sheep in the Faroe Islands, living in the outfields – the fields up in the hills, as opposed to the fields close to the villages – where they find food for themselves. In some places, sheep may come into the fields around villages in the winter, and you may well come across one or two in between the houses. Sheep arrived in the Faroes in about AD 500. They have always been very important for their milk, wool and meat – the oldest surviving document in the Faroe Islands, the 'Sheep Letter', or *Fårebrevet*, of 1298, concerns the organization of sheep farming, among other things. Many households in the Faroes today have a connection with sheep and agriculture but mainly as a hobby. However, there are some who still make a living from sheep farming.

Faroese sheep have short tails and are relatively small. They are known as Northern European short-tailed sheep, part of a breed group originating in the British Isles and the Nordic and Baltic countries. The wool of Faroese sheep has two layers – a soft undercoat with coarse outer guard hairs – which combine to keep sheep warm and dry in the harsh Faroese climate. Faroese wool is particularly rich in lanolin, which means the yarn provides good insulation and is both self-cleaning and water-repellent.

Almost every part of the sheep is eaten. The meat is traditionally hung in a storehouse to dry or ferment, with some meat being eaten fresh. Other parts of the sheep are also eaten, including the liver, kidneys, heart, blood in the form of a type of black pudding, whole sheep's heads and stuffed intestines.

Faroese women were good at multi-tasking. In the old days, when the cows were in the outfields in summer, the milkmaids took their knitting with them when they went out to milk the cows and knitted as they walked.

Kristian and Símun á Torkilsheyggi

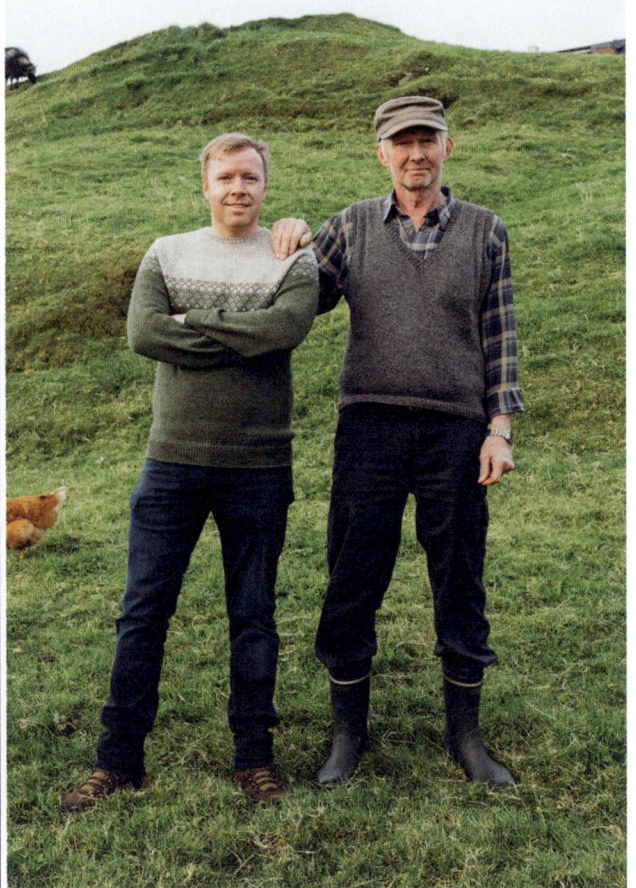

Óli Kristian and Leivur á Torkilsheyggi

TORKILSHEYGSGARÐUR

The old farm of Torkilsheygsgarður in the village of Nes is an important base for Navia. The farm is several hundred years old and has been in the same family for many generations. In 1905, Óli Kristian's great-grandfather got a job at Borðan on Nólsoy and sold half the farm. However, in 2010 the land that had been sold became part of Torkilsheygsgarður again and returned to the family.

Óli Kristian's father, Leivur á Torkilsheyggi, took over the farm when he was just 22 years old and has been running it now for more than 45 years, together with his wife, Elin á Torkilsheyggi. As the eldest of siblings, it is likely that Óli Kristian, the founder of Navia, will take over the farm from his father. However, the farm is nothing without its family. With a stock of over 200 sheep, Torkilsheygsgarður is the natural place for the family to come together. Parents, siblings, spouses, children, cousins and other family members participate in the work of the farm – young and old work together on Torkilsheygsgarður and the farm unites the generations.

At about the age of two, children are allowed to take part in rounding up sheep. As time goes by, they are given bigger jobs and more responsibility and by the age of 13 they have enough experience to be included in the round-up team on an equal footing with adults. Children, adults and the elderly all play important roles in farm work.

Torkilsheygsgarður's outfields are found in three areas: about 50 sheep are located in Húshagi, which is close to Toftir and Nes, and the other 150 are in Yvir í Haga and Nevið, near Rituvík. In the past there were also cattle on Torkilsheygsgarður, but now only sheep remain.

Up in the hills everyone lends a hand with rounding up
and shearing the sheep.

THE TORKILSHEYGSGARÐUR SHEEP

Winter

At Torkilsheygsgarður the sheep year starts on 7 January. On this date, the rams that have been in the outfields to breed with the ewes are brought back to the farm. This is also the season when sheep in the outfields are given extra hay – especially when the weather is cold and snowy. The hay is taken to a barn where the sheep usually seek shelter.

Spring

The first round up of the year takes place in late March. Ewes are given medication to protect them and their lambs from various diseases – this also protects lambs during the first few weeks after birth.

Lambing starts in late April. At this time, the folk from Torkilsheygsgarður are in the outfields every day to make sure that the ewes and lambs are thriving, because there is a risk that any ewes suffering with milk fever will die if they lie down for a long time. Ewes with twin lambs are brought down to the village where there is more grass, which increases milk production.

Summer

In mid-July, the sheep are shorn, given medication and lambs are tagged. At Torkilsheygsgarður shearing is done mainly by hand. They do have electric shears as well, but the traditional sheep shears are used most often.

The date for shearing is decided on when the new wool has grown enough to make the old wool easy to remove. A cool spring and late plant growth delays the growth of new wool so there is no point in bringing the sheep in for shearing if the wool isn't ready.

The sheep stands on a support, while two people carefully cut off the wool – both children and adults help with this job. The wool is cleaned, sorted by colour and then carried home to the farm in bags.

The end of July sees the start of haymaking. At Torkilsheygsgarður they prefer dried hay, but if the weather is bad for drying, the remaining grass is wrapped in bales and stored for the winter. Haymaking is time-consuming and takes most of August, but this is all part of the way of life with sheep and farming.

Autumn

Mid-October is the time for the autumn round-up. This is when the lambs which will be kept for future breeding are selected. Most ewes are sent back to the outfields, but the oldest have to be culled. Typically, this will be 130–150 sheep and everybody lends a hand with the process. On Torkilsheygsgarður the meat is hung in the storehouse (*hjallur* in Faroese) to ferment or dry.

Christmas

On 23 December, at Torkilsheygsgarður the farmer goes out to the storehouse and brings in a piece of wind-dried meat for the first sample to be tasted. It is usually a small shoulder that is not yet completely hard, but there is always something very special about tasting the first bite of that year's meat.

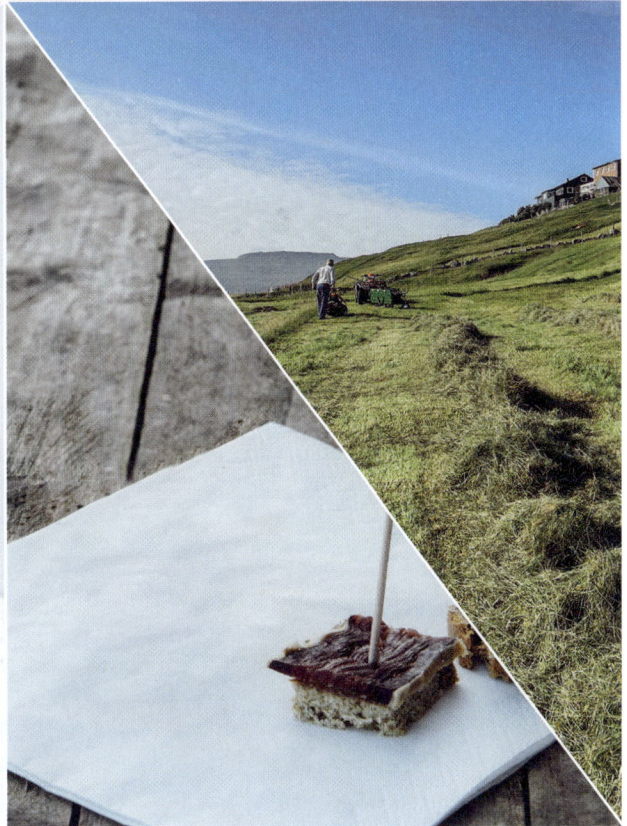

THE PERFECT SHEEP

In the autumn the lambs to be kept for breeding are selected and ewe lambs are in a privileged position because they will bear the lambs that will ensure the future of the flock.

Ewe lambs
For a lamb to survive the selection process, it has to be a reasonably big ewe with nice strong legs. The wool must be good, smooth and even, with little or no parting along the middle of the back, and not be the same colour as all the others – at Torkilsheygsgarður they prefer to have a wide range of sheep colours. It is also important that the lamb's mother is well-behaved. If she is difficult during herding and jumps over the fences, the lamb has no chance. It also matters which flock in the outfields it belongs to, as not all lambs can stay where they were.

Ram lambs
Unfortunately, a ram lamb is already in a worse position than a ewe, just because of its sex. Torkilsheygsgarður needs only eight to eleven ram lambs, so a ram has to try really hard in order to be selected. Firstly, it must be big and have good horns so it can beat any other rams if it comes to a fight. Strong hind legs and good posture are a must, and of course the farmer must like the look of the lamb. Even if all this is fine, the lamb needs genes that are resistant to scrapie disease. What's more, it may also lose out to rams from another farm, as farmers like to have new blood in their outfield flock every year. However, this arrangement works both ways, as the lamb may be moved to another farm.

Ewes
Ewes can relax until they are seven, provided that they have produced some lambs. To last longer than that they have to be lucky, have all their teeth intact, not be thin, produce good lambs and be well-behaved.

In short, if you're a lamb and you want to be selected, you must:

- Look nice
- Have good wool
- Behave well
- Cross your hooves and hope for the best!

FAROESE KNITTING

CULTURE

KNITTING TRADITIONS

We don't know when the Faroese first began to knit. In the Viking period (*c.* 800–1050) people wore clothes made using the ancient technique of *nålebinding*, (also known as single-needle knitting) that predates both knitting and crochet. However, written sources tell us that in 1584 knitted Faroese stockings were used as a means of payment, which means that knitting was common in the Faroe Islands before that date. One thing we do know is that plenty of knitting has been done in the Faroes. In the old days, when the cows were in the outfields in summer, milkmaids knitted as they walked when they went out to milk the cows (see pages 18 and 19). Another activity the Faroese have enjoyed for a good many years is the tradition of knitting clubs.

Knitting clubs

These are an important part of social life in the Faroese community. A knitting club is an informal network, typically a group of women, who meet in turn at each others' homes to knit and chat. It is not unusual for Faroese women who move abroad to set up a knitting club with other expat Faroese to create a network and social bond in their new country. Knitting clubs have other functions as well. For example, they may provide support and help with important birthdays, weddings, funerals and other significant life events. This help often includes baking cakes, cooking, serving food and washing up. Some knitting clubs also arrange social occasions such as parties, foreign travel or communal visits to concerts. The knitting clubs in the Faroe Islands probably started before the Second World War. In Denmark they had so-called sewing clubs, and these came to the Faroes in the 1920s with Faroese girls who had worked as maids in Danish homes. After a time, the sewing clubs in the Faroes turned into knitting clubs – probably because knitting was so widespread in the Islands.

SCHOOL SWEATERS

If you look at a class photo of Faroese children on their first day at school, you will see that the great majority are wearing knitted sweaters. This is because it is traditional in the Faroes to knit sweaters for children when they are about to start their first year of primary school or pre-school. There is no specific definition of what makes a proper school sweater – it can be in any colour, design and pattern. However, boys' sweaters tend to be knitted in traditional Faroese patterns and natural colours, such as grey, dark brown, light brown and white, whereas girls' sweaters are often more colourful, although they also use natural colours. After the first day at school these sweaters are used for everyday wear both at school and at home. It is usually one of the women in the family who knits the school sweater, say the child's mother or one of their grandmothers, but it may also be another person in the family, such as an aunt. The child is often allowed to decide what the school sweater should look like.

THE PATTERNS

It was almost a matter of luck that the old Faroese knitting patterns survived. They were close to disappearing a hundred years ago as the Faroese had begun to knit a lot of items in single colours, probably because they wanted to be able to knit faster in order to produce more garments. In 1932, Hans Marius Debes, known as 'Skrædder' – or Tailor – Debes, published the book *Færøske Strikkemønstre (Faroese Knitting Patterns)*. It was Queen Alexandrine of Denmark, the wife of Christian X, who prompted Debes to collect and publish the Faroese patterns. After an exhibition in 1929 at the Danish Technological Institute in Copenhagen, where some Faroese patterns were displayed, the Queen had been fascinated by the designs and suggested that they should be published. The first edition contained 125 sweater patterns Debes had collected that had been common in the past but which were used less and less often. Before the book came out, the patterns were preserved only in a few old garments and in the memories of elderly people in various parts of the country. However, the old patterns were saved in Skrædder Debes' book and nowadays they are in frequent use for both everyday sweaters and for the Faroese national costume.

WOOL IS GOLD

There is an old saying that 'wool is the gold of the Faroes'. Historically speaking, wool has had great importance for the Faroese, as knitted garments were their main export for a long time and knitted stockings and sweaters were the basis of the economy. The export of knitted stockings started in the mid-17th century, while sweaters were a later addition. This enabled the islanders to import essential goods such as grain. In the second half of the 18th century 120,000 pairs of stockings were exported every year. At that time the annual export of sweaters was only 350 but by the mid-19th century, that had grown to 67,000, while the export of stockings fell considerably. A whole family would participate in the production of woollen goods. Typically, the men spun the wool, while the women knitted. Even people who did not own land or sheep were able to acquire wool by going up into the outfields and collecting the tufts of wool lost by sheep.

Wool was more important than meat, so it was vital to have many sheep – even though in some places there wasn't enough food for them. To collect the wool, farmers went to the outfields twice a year to shear sheep – unlike today, when they are shorn only once a year.

In the years between 1767 and 1776, woollen goods constituted 96.5 per cent of Faroese exports. Between 1841 and 1850 this fell to 60 per cent and in the second half of the 19th century, the Faroese began fishing commercially in small sailing boats, which meant that wool became less economically significant and fish became the new gold of the Faroes.

NAVIA

HISTORY

Navia was founded in 2004 and originally began as a business school project for 22-year-old Óli Kristian á Torkilsheyggi, who is the founder and CEO of Navia.

Navia is a family-run company that continues a long tradition of sheep-rearing and wool-spinning. Óli Kristian's great-grandmother, Suffía Gregersen, employed women to knit for her and sold sweaters in the village of Syðrugøta, where the family had a spinning mill. The farm of Torkilsheygsgarður in Nes, with its flock of 200 sheep, came through his father's family, so Óli learned about wool at an early age.

Óli Kristian founded Navia in an old grocery store in the village of Toftir with no more than 2,000 kroner (roughly £225/US$292) in his pocket. The first items produced by the company were 1-, 2- and 3-ply yarns in six natural colours and a small amount of plain-coloured sock wool. These were sold to yarn shops, cottage industry associations and others who dealt with yarn, and even to small supermarkets all over the country.

In the years that followed Navia grew bigger and produced a wider range of yarns. A new knitting book came out each year and more colours were added, including bright blue, yellow, red and green. This colourful Faroese yarn was a new departure and became very popular.

Navia soon entered the foreign market, where countries like Denmark thought it was novel and interesting to have yarn from the Faroes. From the start, the marketing strategy was to sell the yarn abroad, since the Faroese market on its own is too small.

Since 2004 Navia has grown from a one-man enterprise with only a few different types of yarn to a big company producing clothes, exporting yarn and with two shops selling a wide range of goods.

In 2009, Navia opened a yarn store in Toftir and started producing sweaters. In 2011 the company acquired a unit in the SMS shopping centre in the Faroese capital, Tórshavn, and an old shop, *Oyrahandilin*, in Toftir, which now houses its office, shop and factory.

Large parts of the production and spinning also take place abroad, but on acquiring its new 3D knitting machines Navia moved quite a lot of the knitting back to the Faroe Islands. Technological progress in this area may perhaps make it possible to move all the manufacturing to the Faroes one day.

YARN

Faroese yarn is among the finest there is and, even though there are many other types of wool in the current range, Faroese wool is still the cornerstone for Navia.

Twenty years ago, the range consisted only of the original three yarns Uno, Duo and Trio in six natural colours and a plain-coloured sock wool. Today, Navia has a total of 12 different yarn types in all colours. Navia has a wide range of yarns based on sheep's wool, but we have added other types of yarn fibre, such as alpaca, mohair and a silk-wool blend. People in the Faroes are very knowledgeable about knitting and handicrafts, so we obviously need to include other types of yarn in the Navia family. Using wool from animals that don't live in the Faroe Islands is not unusual and many other yarn manufacturers in the Nordic countries use alpaca and mohair yarn, even though alpacas and angora goats do not naturally live there.

We have kept the classic Navia yarn, which is a mixture of Faroese, Shetland and Australian sheep's wool – a really good combination that produces a soft, hard-wearing yarn that doesn't pill. Used together, the outer guard hairs and the undercoat create a play of colours not found in other types of yarn. However, Faroese yarn can feel scratchy on delicate skin, so among our newest yarns Navia has developed Tradition and Brushed Tradition, which are 100 per cent Faroese wool. Both yarns are reminiscent of the wool used for the traditional Faroese seaman's sweaters, but Tradition includes wool from both the outer and inner coats, whereas seaman's sweater yarn contains only the outer wool. In this case, the Brushed version can provide a solution to the scratchy feeling, as brushing makes the wool softer.

If you are wearing 100 per cent Faroese wool, the weather is always good, even if it is cold, snowy or blowing a gale!

Navia yarns

Uno – *50g/1¾oz/350m/382yd, 100% wool*

Duo – *50g/1¾oz/180m/196yd, 100% wool*

Trio – *50g/1¾oz/120m/131yd, 100% wool*

Sock wool – *50g/1¾oz/120m/131yd, 70% wool,*
30% nylon

Silkiull (Silk wool) – *50g/1¾oz/190m/207yd,*
75% wool, 25% silk

Alpakka – *25g/⅞oz/230m/251yd, 100% alpaca*

Fípa – *50g/1¾oz/90m/98yd, 73% mohair, 22% wool,*
5% nylon

Tradition – *50g/1¾oz/180m/196yd, 100% Faroese wool*

Brushed Tradition – *50g/1¾oz/150m/164yd);*
or 100g/3½oz/300m/328yd,
100% Faroese wool

SUSTAINABILITY

Right from the start, Navia's lifeblood has been a comprehensive selection of knitting yarns and interesting patterns for people with creative hands. But much has happened over the last 20 years and the range has expanded considerably, with Navia now producing sweaters and other knitted garments. The clothes are designed with care and draw inspiration from the Faroese landscape and traditions. Some of our production is carried out using new technology, namely 3D knitting machines, which have revolutionized the knitting process. They work speedily and sustainably and have made it possible to manufacture in the Faroes again. The first machine, bought in 2021, was the first of its kind in the entire kingdom of Denmark. It produced such good results that Navia bought two more.

These machines can knit an adult sweater in just 50 minutes. No cutting and sewing is required because the machine knits the entire garment in one operation. There is only one strand of yarn to be fastened off and the garment is more comfortable to wear because it has no seams. With traditional knitting machines, about 25 per cent of the material goes to waste, since the various parts of the garment are knitted individually, cut to shape and sewn together: with 3D knitting machines, there is no waste.

The new machines require very few people to operate them, so Navia has been able to move large parts of its production back to the Faroe Islands. Knitting at Toftir, the home of Navia, makes it easier to monitor production. Popular items can be quickly produced in larger numbers and, in return, Navia avoids being left with large quantities of unsold clothing. This results in more flexible and sustainable production, in line with the European Union's green transition initiative.

INSPIRATION

Great-grandmother Suffía

Family means a lot to Navia and Óli Kristian's family was a huge source of inspiration for the establishment of the company. His great-grandmother, Suffía Gregersen, was an entrepreneur who started a wool business in Syðrugøta. She and his great-grandfather, Jógvan Elias Gregersen, made a good team. He was a businessman with an understanding of accounting and economics; she was the entrepreneur and very hardworking. Back in the 1930s, Suffía engaged a few women to knit sweaters. They delivered the sweaters to the Gregersens' shop in Syðrugøta and received payment in kind for the work. Great-grandmother's business created a lot of work for local women. During the 1950s, however, the number of spinning mills in the Faroe Islands declined and it became harder to obtain enough yarn for Suffía's knitting business. In 1961 her son Ólavur Gregersen set up the wool company Tøtingarvirkið in Syðrugøta for both spinning and knitting. As time went on, many women went out to work and machines took over the knitting. By the 1980s, fisherman's sweaters were not as popular and Tøtingarvirkið met with challenging times. Production ceased for a few years, but started up again in the 1990s under the new name of Tøting and eventually became the foundation for the creation of Navia.

The thread running through the story of Navia was actually spun by the entrepreneurial family in Syðrugøta, starting with this innovative great-grandmother.

Auntie Elsa

What do you do if you have ordered 200 sweaters to sell at the G! rock festival and suddenly discover that the neck band on all of them is too tight? You phone Auntie Elsa, of course. It is five years since Auntie Elsa saved Navia's G! festival by unravelling all the neckbands and knitting new ones. She is now 90 years old, but she's still a great help. Elsa Nielsen is Óli Kristian's great aunt, but everybody calls her Auntie Elsa.

Auntie Elsa grew up with wool in her mother's knitting business with all the local women who sat knitting in the living room, while the men were spinning in the kitchen and people up in the loft were carding the wool. All the garments they knitted were hung to dry on the radiators and then pressed. Then all the goods were packed up in the kitchen and living room. Auntie Elsa and her sisters were responsible for all the household chores such as baking, washing, tidying up and providing food for the workers. The sisters also had the job of looking after the knitters' children.

Auntie Elsa was only seven years old when she knitted her first sweater and she worked in the Tøtingarvirkið and Tøting wool companies for many years, knitting and finishing the dark red-brown sweaters and underwear – a job she very much enjoyed. For many years, the knitting machine was called Elsa.

When Óli Kristian started Navia 20 years ago he often asked Auntie Elsa for advice, and he still does so today. She advised him to start small, build up the business step by step and weed out items from old collections when new ones went on the market, so there would not be too much stock lying around. Even though the new knitting machines are very advanced, Navia also needed guidance from Auntie Elsa, this time in order to streamline the technique of fastening off the ends of yarn in the sweaters.

'Every step takes time: picking up the yarn, threading it through the needle, sewing it in and cutting it off. It's very important not to waste time.' – Auntie Elsa.

KNITTING PATTERNS
AND DESIGNS

Today's knitters are very choosy. There is great demand for good design and finish, and everything must be perfect, so it is important to have patterns that will interest experienced knitters as well as simpler ones that anyone can knit. Inspiration for Navia's designs comes from all sorts of places – from classic Faroese patterns to everyday ideas, such as birthdays, holidays, Pinterest and so on. Most of Navia's knitting patterns are designed by friends Sára Mrdalo and Tóra Joensen, who have been responsible for our patterns for many years.

In the early years of Navia, creating patterns could be difficult. The company held knitting competitions but many of the entrants just improvised their designs and didn't keep any notes of what they did as they were knitting. The two designers, therefore, had to use a lot of ingenuity to work out how the winning sweaters were knitted. Sometimes it was almost impossible, for example if the sweater had been felted.

Patterns with a theme

Nowadays Navia publishes ten small knitting booklets every year with four or five patterns in each, whereas they previously issued two bigger booklets with a mixture of 16 assorted models. Today's booklets have various themes such as baby clothes, shawls, Trom sweaters, minimalism or particular yarns.

The photos of the various designs are taken with care, with great emphasis on finding the right locations and models for the shoot.

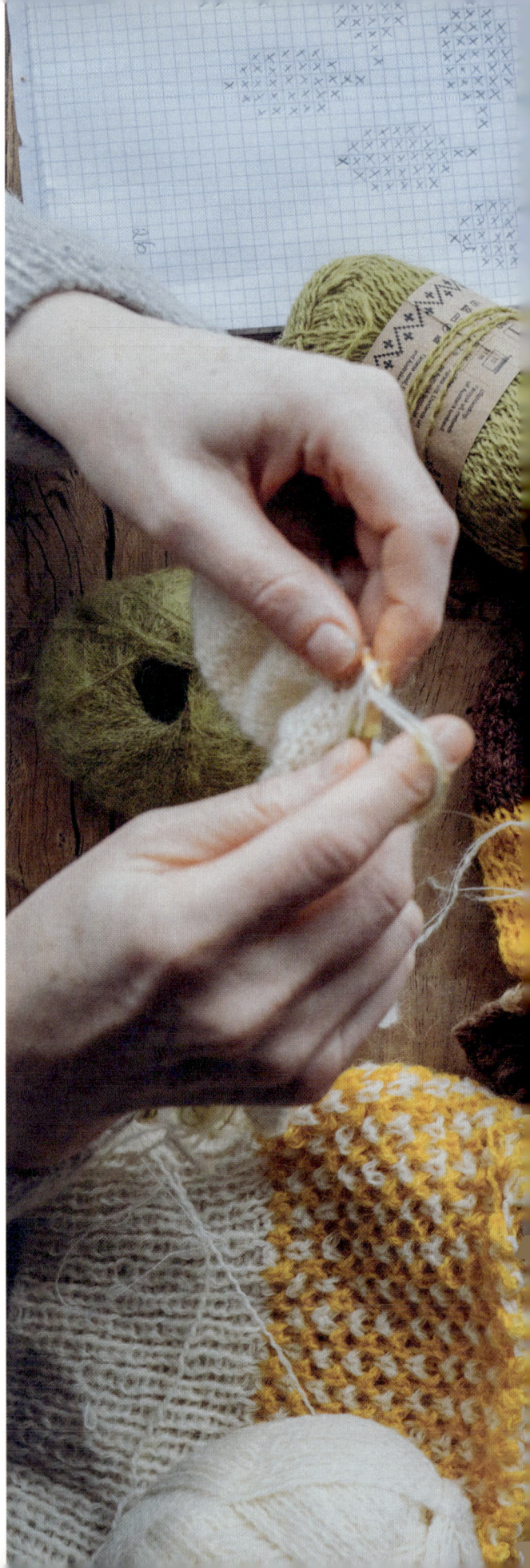

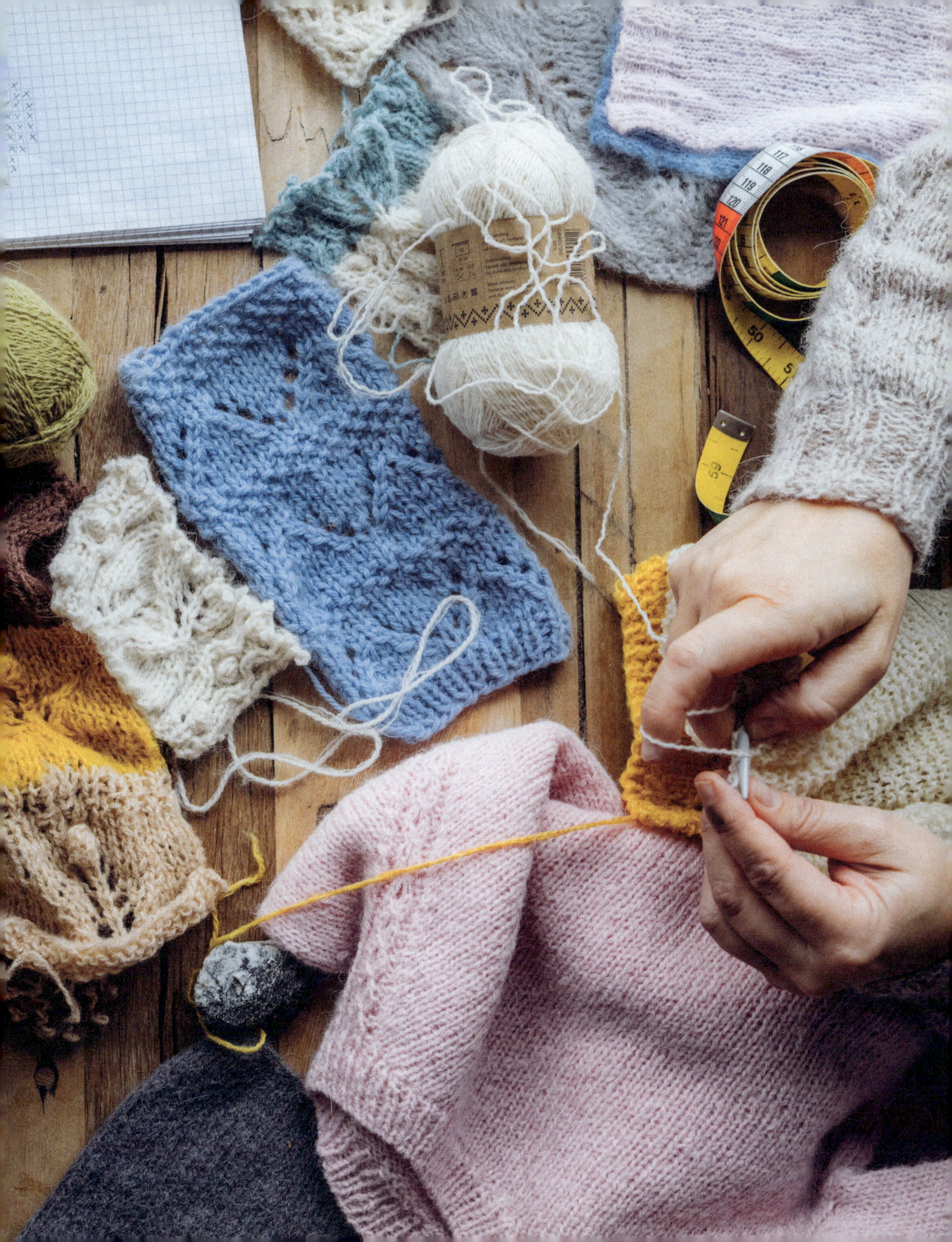

THE PEOPLE BEHIND NAVIA

Paula á Torkilsheyggi (graphic designer)
Paula, Óli Kristian's wife, is responsible for the patterns and layout of all the knitting booklets as well as designing the ball bands for the yarn, drawing up advertisements and sketching sweater designs. She also has a good eye for attractive creative displays in shops. While the family tries not to talk about Navia outside of working hours, it is usually not long before yarn shades, sweater designs and knitting machines once again become the topic of conversation during the evening meal!

Tóra Eyðunsson (shop assistant)
Tóra is one of the first people to be employed by Navia. She started working with us in 2009 when the first yarn shop opened in Toftir and she currently works in the store in Tórshavn's SMS shopping centre. Although Tóra is not a member of the Torkilsheyggi family, she is still an extremely important part of Navia, and is now thought of as part of the family.

Erla á Torkilsheyggi Djurhuus (shop manager)
Erla, the eldest of Óli Kristian's sisters, has been permanently employed at Navia for the last eight years and manages the Navia stores in SMS in Tórshavn and in Toftir, where she is mainly found. She is a trained sales assistant, and twice a year she accompanies Óli Kristian to sales fairs in Denmark, where they sell yarn to Danish retailers. Erla also usually takes over the management tasks when Óli Kristian is away.

Óluva á Torkilsheyggi (marketing manager)
Óluva, the youngest sister, knows about almost everything at Navia and is the one that others call on when they need help. She is trained in marketing management and was appointed to a permanent position five years ago. She deals chiefly with marketing, the online store and social media, as well as updating the website and packing orders for the web shop. Since the 3D knitting machines arrived, Óluva has looked after them alongside Óli Kristian.

Beinta á Torkilsheyggi (photographer)

Beinta, the middle sister, is Navia's photographer. Trained in photography, she takes the pictures for most of the knitting booklets as well as dealing with campaign images for the website, banners and so on. Beinta is a perfectionist and won't stop until an image is just as it should be.

Sára Mrdalo and Tóra Joensen (knitwear designers)

Friends Sára and Tóra are Navia's knitwear designers and have been with the company almost from the start. Sára coordinates the models for the knitting booklets and designs many of them herself. She and our knitters write down the details of how they make the garment and these notes are then passed on to Tóra along with the sweater they have knitted. Tóra draws up the instructions, calculates the sizes and creates the charts, and then everything is sent off for proofreading. Together, Sára and Tóra have created countless patterns, some of them quite challenging.

Óli Kristian á Torkilsheyggi (founder and CEO of Navia)

In one way or another Óli Kristian á Torkilsheyggi has always known that his occupation would be something to do with wool. He grew up with yarn, spinning and knitting, and he began working for the wool company Tøting in Syðrugøta at the age of just 13 – his first job was putting the labels on skeins of yarn. Later he worked in the shop and then with the knitting machines. When the other boys were playing football after school, Óli Kristian went to work. He was fascinated by wool, especially by the process whereby the raw material – wool taken from the sheep that might be dirty and smelly – was transformed into a finished product. After business college, Óli Kristian went to Denmark to study for a degree in marketing management. His project for his finals was about a company called Navia, which officially became a yarn manufacturer on 7 January 2004.

THE NAVIA PATTERNS

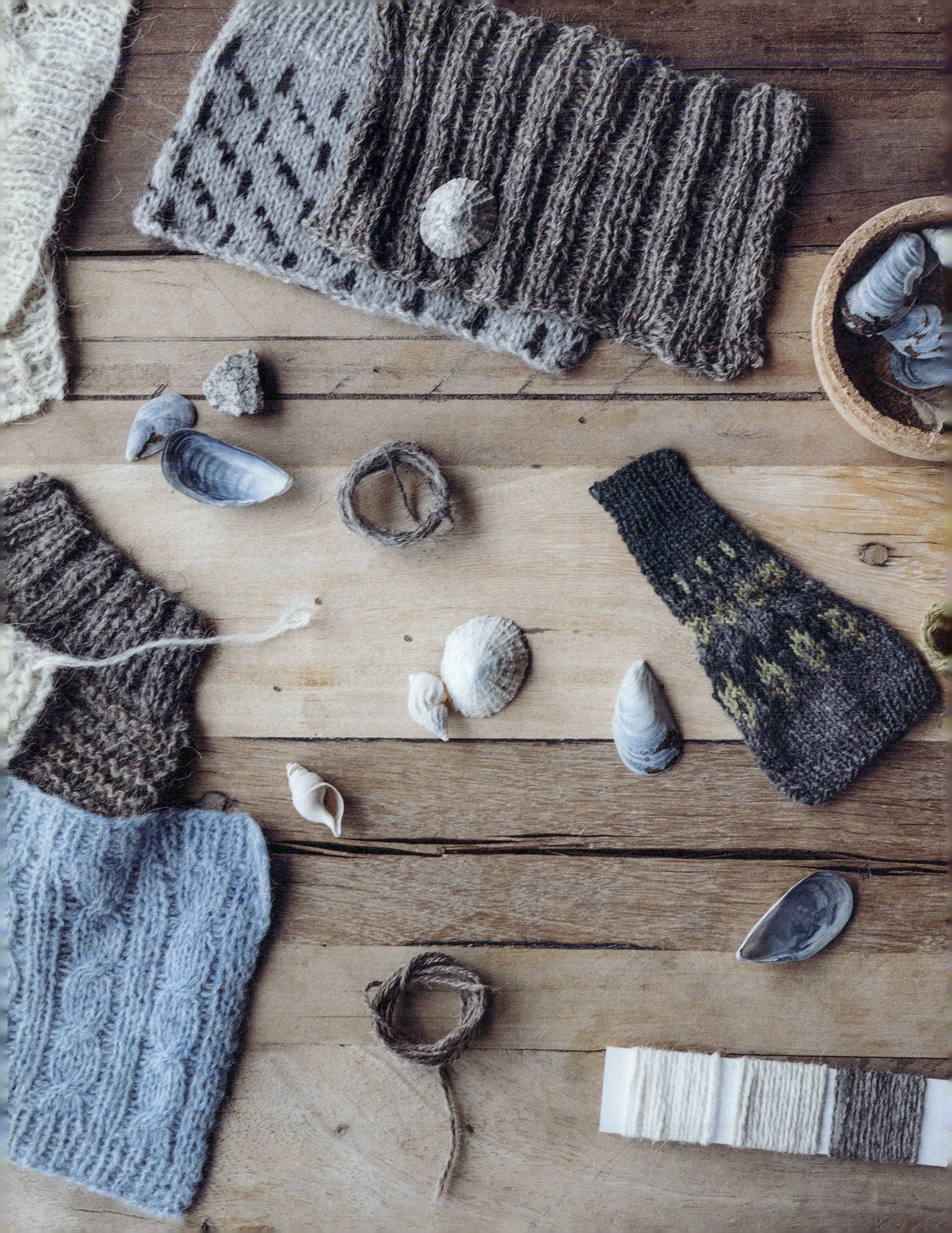

ABBREVIATIONS:

alt = alternate(ly)

beg = begin(ning)

brk = brioche knit

brp = brioche purl

cont = continu(e)/(ing)

dec = decreas(e)/(ed)/(ing)

DPN = double pointed needles

foll = follow(s)/(ing)

g st = garter stitch

inc = increas(e)/(ing)

k2tog = knit 2 sts together

k3tog = knit 3 sts together

k = knit

p = purl

M = stitch marker

PM = place stitch marker

psso = pass the slipped st(s) over

rep = repeat

rev st st = reverse stocking (stockinette) stitch (p on RS, k on WS)

RS = right side

skpo = sl1, k1, psso

sl = slip(ped)

st(s) = stitch(es)

st st = stocking (stockinette) stitch

tbl = through the back loop

tog = together

WS = wrong side

yo = yarn over

yrn = yarn round needle

ytb = yarn to back

ytf = yarn to front

CROCHET STITCHES

ch = chain stitch

ch sp = chain space

dc = double crochet (US = single crochet)

sl st = slip stitch (crochet)

tr = treble crochet (US = double crochet)

Tension (gauge)

Tension (gauge) is provided per project. It is important to keep to the right tension (gauge): the needles listed per project are a suggestion: if the given number of stitches results in less than 10cm (4in), change to larger needles. If the given number of stitches results in more than 10cm (4in), change to smaller needles.

Difficulty ratings

These are given on a scale of one to five stars, with one being suitable for beginners and five for very experienced knitters.

LEAF-PATTERN CARDIGAN

pattern: model 1 – NB51 (on www.navia.fo)

design: Sára Mrdalo

LEAF-PATTERN
CARDIGAN

Difficulty * * *

Sizes XS(S/M:M:L)

Bust 86(92:98:104)cm / 33¾(36¼:38½:41)in

Length 54(58:62:66)cm / 21¼(22¾:24½:26)in

Yarn Navia Alpakka (25g/⅞oz); in White (801)

Quantity 7(8:9:10) balls

Suggested needles 3mm and 4mm (UK 11 and 8, US 2–3 and 6) circular needles, 60 or 80cm (24 or 32in) long
3mm and 4mm (UK 11 and 8, US 2–3 and 6) DPN
2.5mm (UK 12, US C/2) crochet hook

Notions 9 buttons (for all sizes)
Stitch holders

Tension (gauge) 19.5 sts in st st using 4mm (UK 8, US 6) needles = 10cm (4in)

Note This cardigan is knitted using two strands of Navia Alpakka held together. The leaf pattern is worked along both front edges and on the sleeves. The back is worked in stocking (stockinette) stitch. The cardigan has slightly puffed sleeves.

Washing Wash the garment in a suitable wool detergent. After washing, spread it out on a towel to dry.

Back and Front Using 3mm (UK 11, US 2–3) circular needle and two strands of yarn, cast on 168(180:192:204) sts and work 16 rows in k1, p1 rib. Change to 4mm (UK 8, US 6) circular needle and set the position of the pattern as foll: work 15 sts of chart 2, k138(150:162:174), work 15 sts of chart 3.
Cont in this way, maintaining pattern on either side of a st st panel and without shaping until work measures 32(35:38:41)cm / 12½(13¾:15:16¼)in, ending on a WS row.
Divide for Back and Fronts as foll: work 38(41:44:47) sts (15 sts from chart 2, k23(26:29:32)), cast off (bind off) 8 sts, k76(82:88:94), cast off (bind off) 8 sts, work 38(41:44:47) sts (k23(26:29:32), 15 sts from chart 3).
Transfer the 38(41:44:47) sts on either side of your work to st holders, then rejoin yarn to centre 76(82:88:94) sts and cont for Back.

Back Shape armholes as foll: cast off (bind off) 1 st at both armhole edges on every other row until 66(72:78:84) sts rem.
Cont in st st without further shaping until Back measures 22(23:24:25)cm / 8¾(9:9½:9¾)in from armholes.
Cast off (bind off).

Right Front Place sts back on needles, rejoin yarn and cont working the pattern panel from chart 2 and in st st, while at the same time casting off 1 st at armhole edge on every other row five times (33(36:39:42) sts).
Work without shaping until Right Front measures 47(48:49:50)cm / 18½(19:19¼:19¾)in, finishing with a complete leaf (pattern rep).
Work a RS row, dec over sts of the pattern panel as foll: p2, (k2tog, k1) three times, k2tog, p2 (pattern panel has now been reduced to 11 sts).
P 1 row.
Shape neck as foll: cast off (bind off) 9 sts, then cast off (bind off) 1 st three(four:six:seven) times at neck edge on every other row (17(19:20:22) sts).
Work without shaping until Right Front measures same as Back.
Cast off (bind off).
Join Right Front and Back at shoulder.

Left Front As for Right Front, working from chart 3 and reversing shaping for neck.

Sleeves (make 2)   Using 3mm (UK 11, US 2–3) DPN and two strands of yarn, cast on 36(36:38:38) sts and work 16 rounds in k1, p1, rib.
Change to 4mm (UK 8, US 6) DPN and k 1 round, inc evenly by 11(13:13:15) sts over the round (47(49:51:53) sts).
Set the position of the pattern with st st panels on either side as foll: work 10(11:12:13) sts in st st, 27 sts of chart 1, 10(11:12:13) sts in st st.
Cont in this way, and at the same time inc by 1 st at both beg and end of round on every eighth(eighth:seventh:seventh) round until you have 61(67:73:79) sts.
Cont until Sleeve measures 42(43:44:44)cm / 16½(17:17¼:17¼)in.
Cast off (bind off) 4 sts each at end of the round and beg of foll round. Then cont on rem 53(59:65:71) sts, now working in rows, to shape Sleeve cap as foll: dec by 1 st at both beg and end of every fourth row until 33(37:41:45) sts rem; end with a WS row.
Work 1 row, dec in pattern only, as foll: k3(5:7:9), p2, (k2tog, k1) seven times, k2tog, p2, k3(5:7:9) (25(29:33:37) sts).
Work 1 WS row.
On foll RS row, dec as foll to shape puffed sleeve top: k2, *k2tog, rep from * until 3 sts remain, k3.
Cast off (bind off).

Buttonhole Band   Using 2.5mm (UK 12, US C/2) crochet hook and two strands of yarn, work about 85(92:99:106) dc along the edge of Right Front.
Work 2 rows of dc.
On next row, make eight buttonholes, evenly spaced, as foll: 3 dc, 2 ch, skip 2 dc, *work in dc to position of next buttonhole, 2 ch, skip 2 dc, rep from * until you have made a total of eight buttonholes, ending the row with 3 dc.
Work 2 more rows in dc, making 2 dc in each ch sp, then work a row of sl st. Fasten off.

Button Band   Using 2 strands of yarn and 2.5mm (UK 12, US C/2) crochet hook, work about 85(92:99:106) dc along the edge of Left Front.
Work 5 rows in dc, then work a row of sl st.

Neckband   Using 2.5mm (UK 12, US 2) crochet hook and two strands of yarn, work about 102(108:114:120) dc along edge of neck. Fasten off.
Work 5 rows, making a buttonhole as described above on the third row at the Button Band end of the Neckband.
Work 1 row in crab stitch (a row of dc worked backwards).

Finishing   Sew the sleeves into the armholes. Sew on the buttons to correspond with the buttonholes.

Chart 1: pattern panel for Sleeve

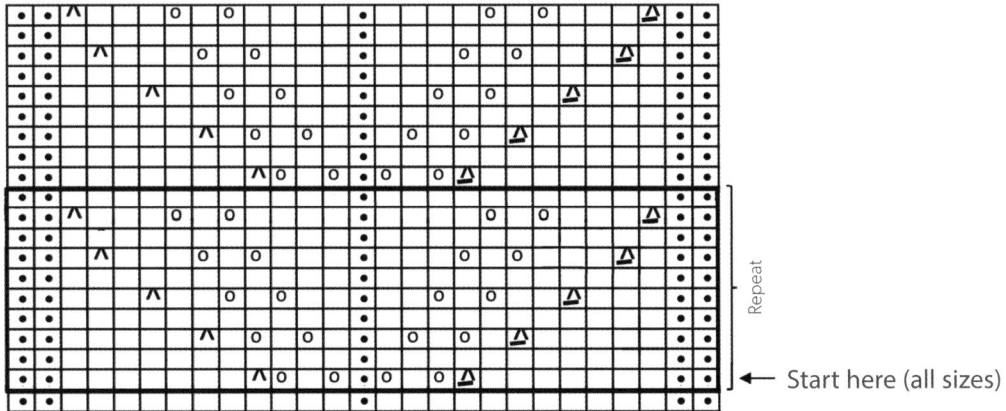

Repeat

← Start here (all sizes)

Chart 2: pattern panel on Right Front

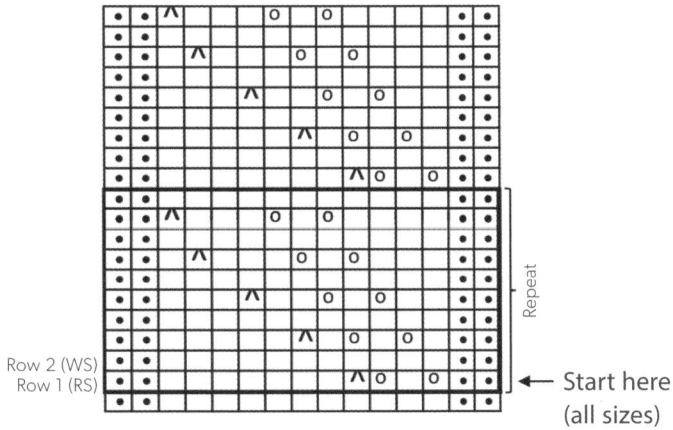

Row 2 (WS)
Row 1 (RS)

Repeat

← Start here
(all sizes)

Chart 3: pattern panel on Left Front

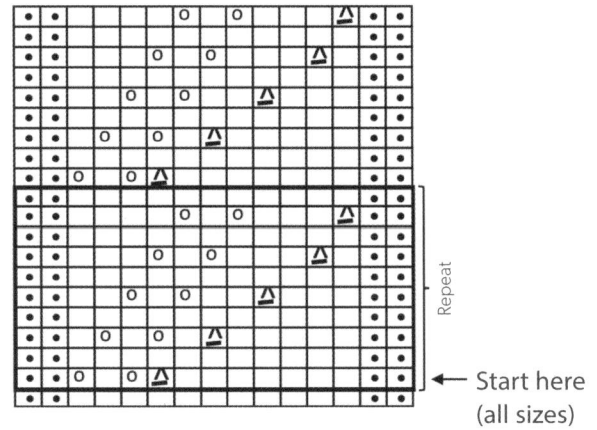

Repeat

← Start here
(all sizes)

☐ k on RS, p on WS

• p on RS, k on WS

O yo

Λ sl1, k2tog, psso

◢ k3tog

CHILD'S LEAF-PATTERN CARDIGAN

pattern: model 3 – NB49 (on www.navia.fo)

design: Sára Mrdalo

CHILD'S LEAF-PATTERN CARDIGAN

Difficulty * * *

Sizes 5(7:9) years

Chest 66(72:79)cm / 26(28¼:31)in

Length 39(45:51)cm /15¼(17¾:20)in

Yarn Navia Alpakka (25g/⅞oz); in White (801)

Quantity 4(4:5) balls

Suggested needles 3.5mm and 4.5mm (UK 10–9 and 7, US 4 and 7) circular needles, 60 or 80cm (24 or 32in) long
3.5mm and 4.5mm (UK 10–9 and 7, US 4 and 7) DPN
2.5mm (UK 12, US C/2) crochet hook

Notions 7 buttons (for all sizes)
Stitch holders

Tension (gauge) 18 sts in st st using 4.5mm (UK 7, US 7) needles = 10cm (4in)

Note This cardigan is knitted using two strands of Navia Alpakka held together. The sleeves are worked from the top down, working in rows for the cap then changing to working in the round.

Washing Wash the garment in a suitable wool detergent. After washing, spread it out on a towel to dry.

Back and Front   Using 3.5mm (UK 10–9, US 4) circular needle and two strands of yarn, cast on 115(127:139) sts and work 13 rows in k1, p1 rib. Change to 4.5mm (UK 7, US 7) circular needle and set the position of the pattern as foll: work 15 sts of chart 1, k85(97:109), work 15 sts of chart 2.
Cont in this way, maintaining pattern on either side of st st panel, without shaping until work measures 22(27:32)cm / 8¾(10¾:12½)in.
Divide for Back and Front as foll: work 26(29:32) sts (15 sts from chart 1, k11(14:17)), cast off (bind off) 6 sts, k51(57:63), cast off (bind off) 6 sts, work 26(29:32) sts (k11(14:17), 15 sts from chart 2).
Transfer the 26(29:32) sts on either side of your work to st holders, then rejoin yarn to centre 51(57:63) sts and cont for Back.

Back   Shape armholes as foll: cast off (bind off) 1 st at both armhole edges on every other row until 45(51:57) sts rem.
Cont in st st without further shaping until Back measures 17(18:19)cm / 6¾(7:7½)in from armholes.
Cast off (bind off).

Right Front   Place sts back on needles, rejoin yarn and cont working the pattern panel from chart 1 and in st st, while at the same time casting off 1 st at armhole edge on every other row three times (23(26:29) sts).
Work without shaping until Right Front measures 31(37:43)cm / 12¼(14½:17)in, finishing with a complete leaf (pattern rep).
Work a RS row, dec over sts of the pattern panel as foll: p2, (k2tog, k1) three times, k2tog, p2.
On next (WS) row, work k2, p7, k2 across the leaf pattern.
Shape neck as foll: cast off (bind off) 9 sts, then cast off (bind off) 1 st three(five:six) times on every other row (7(8:10) sts).
Work without shaping until Right Front measures same as Back.
Cast off (bind off).
Join Right Front and Back at shoulder.

Left Front   As for Right Front, working from chart 2 and reversing shaping for neck.

Sleeve Using 4.5mm (UK 7, US 7) circular needle and two strands of yarn, and with RS facing, pick up and k 16 sts at the top of right armhole (8 sts on either side of shoulder seam) and beg about 5cm (2in) from the seam.

Turn and p 1 row.

Cont to work in rows and in st st, picking up 1 st alt from Back and Right Front at end of each row until there are 56(62:68) sts.

Change to 4.5mm (UK 7, US 7) circular needle and join to work in the round.

Cont to work in st st, dec 2 sts at centre underarm on every fourth round until 28(30:32) sts rem.

Change to 3.5mm (UK 10–9, US 4) DPN and work k1, p1 rib for 13 rounds.

Cast off (bind off).

Rep to add left sleeve.

Buttonhole Band Using 2.5mm (UK 12, US C/2) crochet hook and two strands of yarn, work about 50(60:70) dc along the edge of Right Front.

Work 1 row of dc.

On next row, make six buttonholes, evenly spaced, as foll: 3 dc, 2 ch, skip 2 dc, * work in dc to position of next buttonhole, 2 ch, skip 2 dc, rep from * until you have made a total of six buttonholes, ending the row with 5 dc.

Work 2 more rows in dc, making 2 dc in each ch sp. Fasten off.

Button Band Using 2.5mm (UK 12, US C/2) crochet hook and two strands of yarn, work about 50(60:70) dc along the edge of Left Front.

Work 4 rows in dc. Fasten off.

Neckband Using 2.5mm (UK 12, US 2) crochet hook and two strands of yarn, work about 70(76:82) dc along edge of neck.

Work 4 rows, making a buttonhole as described above on the second row and at the Button-Band end of the neckband.

Work 1 row in crab stitch (a row of dc worked backwards). Fasten off.

Finishing Sew on the buttons to correspond with the buttonholes.

Chart 1: pattern panel on Right Front

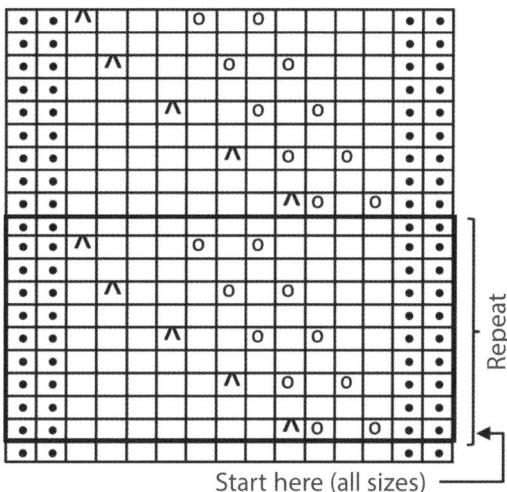

Repeat

Start here (all sizes)

Chart 2: pattern panel on Left Front

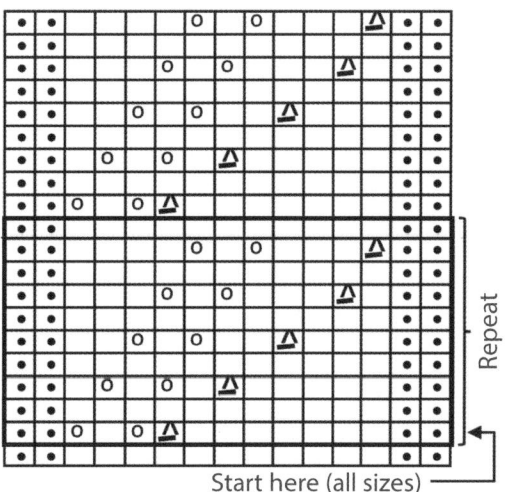

Repeat

Start here (all sizes)

k on RS, p on WS

p on RS, k on WS

yo

sl1, k2tog, psso

k3tog

79

CHILD'S SWEATER WITH RETRO PATTERN

pattern: model 4 – NB66 (on www.navia.fo)

design: Sára Mrdalo

CHILD'S SWEATER WITH RETRO PATTERN

Difficulty * *

Sizes 5(7:9:10) years

Chest 67(73:79:85)cm / 26½(28¾:31:33½)in

Length 38(44:50:57)cm / 15(17¼:19¾:22½)in

Yarn Navia Duo (50g/1¾oz); in Sand (28), Nutmeg (276), Vintage Teak (267) and Stargazer (262)

Quantity
A – Sand, 2(3:4:5) balls
B – Nutmeg, 1 ball for each size
C – Vintage Teak, 1 ball for each size
D – Stargazer, 1 ball for each size

Suggested needles 2.5mm and 3mm (UK 13–12 and 11, US 1–2 and 2–3) circular needles, 60 or 80cm (24 or 32in) long 3mm (UK 11, US 2–3) straight needles 2.5mm and 3mm (UK 13–12 and 11, US 1–2 and 2–3) DPN

Notions Stitch holder or spare yarn

Tension (gauge) 20 sts in st st using 3mm (UK 11, US 2–3) needles = 10cm (4in)

Washing Wash the garment in a suitable wool detergent. After washing, spread it out on a towel to dry.

Back and Front   Using 2.5mm (UK13–12, US 1–2) circular needle and yarn A, use an Italian cast-on (i.e. cast on with a twisted loop rather than a slipknot) to cast on 134(146:158:170) sts and join to work in the round. Work in k1, p1 rib for 3cm (1¼in). Change to 3mm (UK 11, US 2–3) circular needle and cont in st st until work measures about 23(28:33:39) cm / 9(11:13:15¼)in or desired length. Divide for Back and Front as foll: cast off (bind off) 3 sts, k61(67:73:79), cast off (bind off) 6 sts, k61(67:73:79), cast off (bind off) 3 sts. Turn and cont on first 61(67:73:79) sts for Back; transfer rem 61(67:73:79) sts (for Front) to a stitch holder.

Back   Cont in rows, in st st, and shape armholes as foll:
P 1 row.
Dec row (RS): skpo, k to last 2 sts, k2tog.
Rep previous 2 rows until 57(63:69:75) sts rem.
Cont in st st and start working colourwork pattern from chart, and at same time rep Dec row every fourth row until 51(55:59:63) sts rem.
Cont in st st without shaping until Back measures 15(16:17:18)cm / 6(6¼:6¾:7)in from armhole. Cut yarn and place sts on a stitch holder.

Front   Shape neck as foll: k19(20:21:22), turn and work on these sts only for left side of neck.
At neck edge, cast off (bind off) 3 sts at beg of next row, 2 sts at beg of foll alt row, then 1 st at beg of foll 2(3:3:4) rows (12(12:13:13) sts).
Cont without shaping until Left Front measures the same as Back. Cut yarn and place sts on a stitch holder.
Rejoin yarn to rem 32(35:38:41) sts, cast off (bind off) 13(15:17:19) sts, and cont on rem 19(20:21:22) sts for right side of neck.
At neck edge, cast off (bind off) 3 sts at beg of next row, 2 sts at beg of foll alt row, then 1 st at beg of foll 2(3:3:4) rows (12(12:13:13) sts).
Cont without shaping until Right Front measures the same as Back.
Transfer the sts for the Back to a 3mm (UK 11, US 2–3) straight needle, then hold Back and right-hand side of Front RS tog and work a 3-needle cast off (bind off) until all the sts of the Front have been cast off. Use the same technique to join the left-hand side of Front and Back tog. Leave the rem Back sts on stitch holder or spare length of yarn.

Sleeves (make 2) Using 2.5mm (UK13–12, US 1–2) DPN and yarn A, use an Italian cast-on to cast on 38(40:42:44) sts and join to work in the round.
Work in k1, p1 rib for 3cm (1¼in).
Change to 3mm (UK 11, US 2–3) DPN and cont in st st, inc by 1 st on first round (39(41:43:45) sts).
Cont in st st, inc 1 st at both beg and end of a round at 5(5:4.5:4)cm / 2(2:1¾:1½)in intervals three(five:seven:nine) times (45(51:57:63) sts).
Cont without shaping until sleeve measures 28(32:36:38)cm / 11(12½:14¼:15)in or desired length.
Cast off (bind off) 3 sts each at end of the round and beg of foll round. Then cont on rem 39(45:51:57) sts, now working in rows, to shape the sleeve cap as foll.
K2tog at each end of every other row twice (35(41:47:53) sts).

Work from the chart, and at same time k2tog at each end of every fourth row three(four:five:six) times (29(33:37:41) sts).
Work 1 row, then cast off (bind off) 3(3:4:4) sts at beg of next row. Cast off (bind off) 4(4:4:5) sts at beg of next row. Cast off (bind off) 4(5:5:5) sts at beg of next row.

Neckband Using 2.5mm (UK13–12, US 1–2) DPN and yarn A, pick up and k about 76(82:86:90) sts around neckline, including sts from stitch holder for Back and work in k1, p1 rib for 2cm (1in).
Cast off (bind off) with Italian cast-off (bind-off) (i.e. sew together the stitches for a neat finish and stretchy edge).

Finishing Sew the sleeves into the armholes.

Chart

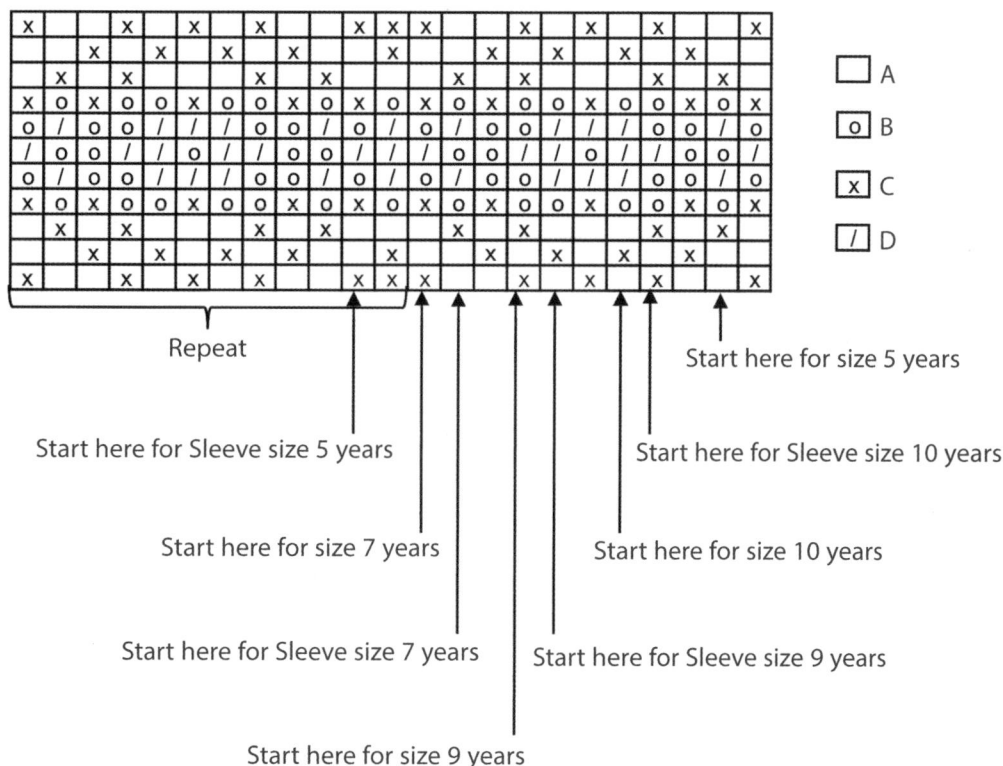

Legend:
- ☐ A
- ⊙ B
- ⊠ C
- ⊘ D

Repeat

Start here for Sleeve size 5 years
Start here for size 7 years
Start here for Sleeve size 7 years
Start here for size 9 years
Start here for Sleeve size 9 years
Start here for size 10 years
Start here for Sleeve size 10 years
Start here for size 5 years

TRADITIONAL SWEATER

pattern: model 4 – NB38 (on www.navia.fo)

design: Navia

TRADITIONAL SWEATER

Difficulty * *

Sizes S(M:L:XL)

Chest/bust 89(100:111:122)cm / 35(39¼:43¾:48)in

Length 66(71:75:79)cm / 26(28:29½:31)in

Yarn Navia Brushed Tradition (50g/1¾oz); in Light Grey (1102), Light Brown (1105) and Dark Brown (1106)

Quantity
A – Light Grey, 6(6:8:10) balls
B – Light Brown, 2(2:4:4) balls
C – Dark Brown, 2(2:4:6) balls

Suggested needles 4mm and 5.5mm (UK 8 and 5, US 6 and 9) circular needles, 60 or 80cm (24 or 32in) long
5.5mm (UK 5, US 9) straight needles
4mm and 5.5mm (UK 8 and 5, US 6 and 9) DPN
(A 4mm (UK 8, US 6) circular needle, 40cm (16in) long, can be used for the neck)

Notions 2 safety pins
Stitch holders

Tension (gauge) 18 sts in st st using 5.5mm (UK 5, US 9) needles = 10cm (4in)

Washing Wash the garment in a suitable wool detergent. After washing, spread it out on a towel to dry.

Back and Front   Using 4mm (UK 8, US 6)circular needle and yarn A, cast on 160(180:200:220) sts and join to work in the round. Work in k2, p2 rib for 5cm (2in).
Change to 5.5mm (UK 5, US 9) circular needle and cont in st st, foll the chart, until work measures 43(47:50:53)cm / 17(18½:19¾:21)in.
Divide for Back and Front as foll: place 1 st on a safety pin, work 79(89:99:109) sts, place next st on a safety pin, work 79(89:99:109) sts.
Turn and cont on first 79(89:99:109) sts for Back; place rem 79(89:99:109) sts (for Front) on a stitch holder.

Back   Cont in st st and foll chart, work in rows without shaping until Back measures 66(71:75:79)cm / 26(28:29½:31)in. Place sts on a stitch holder.

Front   Place Front sts back on needles. Cont in st st and foll chart, work in rows without shaping until Front measures 14(15:16:17)cm / 5½(6:7¼:7¾)in from point where work was divided for Front and Back, ending on a WS row.
Shape neck as foll: k33(37:41:45), turn and work on these sts only for left side of neck.
At same time as working in st st and foll chart, cast off (bind off) 3 sts at beg of next row, 2 sts at beg of foll alt row, 1(1:2:2) st(s) at beg of foll alt row, 1(1:1:2) st(s) at beg of foll alt row (26(30:33:36) sts).
Cont without shaping until left side of Front measures the same as Back, ending on a RS row. Cut yarn, leaving a long tail to work 3-needle cast-off (bind-off) later and place sts on a stitch holder.
With RS facing, transfer next 13(15:17:19) sts to a stitch holder.
Rejoin yarn to rem 33(37:41:45) sts and work dec at neck edge as for left side of neck, and at same time work in st st and foll chart.
Cont without shaping until right side of Front measures the same as Back.
Transfer the sts for the Back to a 5.5mm (UK 5, US 9) straight needle, then hold Back and right-hand side of Front RS tog and work a 3-needle cast off (bind off) until all the sts of the Front have been cast off. Use the same technique to join the left-hand side of Front and Back tog. Leave the rem Back sts on stitch holder.

Sleeve Using 5.5mm (UK 5, US 9) circular needle and yarn A, with RS facing, transfer the st on safety pin at right armhole to the needle, then pick up and k 70(80:90:100) sts around the armhole (71(81:91:101) sts). Divide sts bet 5.5mm (UK 5, US 9) DPN and join to work in the round.

Cont in st st and foll chart, working the st that was on safety pin in yarn A for centre underarm; at same time dec by 2 sts at centre underarm on every fifth(fifth:fourth:fourth) round until 43(49:55:61) sts rem. Work without shaping until sleeve measures 48(52:54:55)cm / 19(20½:21¼:21¾)in.

Change to 4mm (UK 8, US 6) DPN and work 1 round, dec evenly by 1(5:7:13) sts (42(44:48:48) sts).
Cont in k2, p2 rib for 5cm (2in).
Cast off (bind off) in rib.
Rep to add left sleeve.

Neckband Using 4mm (UK 8, US 6) DPN or 40cm (16in) long circular needle and yarn A, pick up and k 76(80:84:88) sts around neckline, including sts from stitch holders for Back and Front and work k2, p2 rib for 20cm (8in).
Cast off (bind off) in rib.

Chart for the pattern

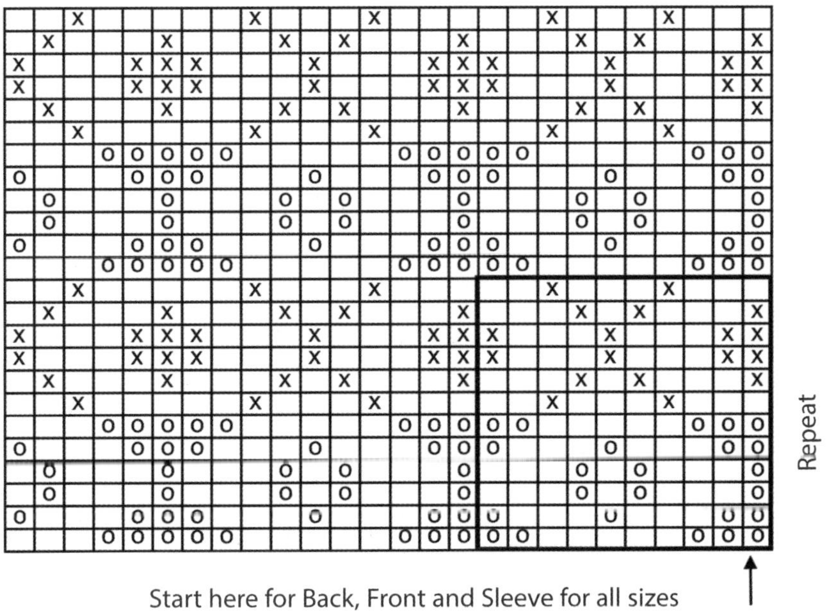

Repeat

Start here for Back, Front and Sleeve for all sizes

☐ A   ☒ B   ⊡ C

87

BABY CLOTHES AND BLANKET

patterns: models 2–3 – NB26 (on www.navia.fo)
design: Sára Mrdalo
design: Gunnvør Frederiksberg

BODYSUIT WITH STAR MOTIF

Difficulty * * *

Sizes 62(68:74:80)cm / 24½(26¾:29¼:31½)in
(baby's total length)

Chest 35(39:44:49)cm / 13¾(15¼:17¼:19¼)in

Length (front of bodysuit): 34(37:40:45)cm /
13½(14½:15¾:17¾)in

Yarn
Navia Uno (50g/1¾oz); in White (11), Pastel
Pink (132) and Mid Grey (13)

Quantity
A – White, 1 ball for each size
B – Pastel Pink, 1 ball for each size
C – Mid Grey, 1 ball for each size

Suggested needles 3mm and 3.5mm (UK 11
and 10–9, US 2–3 and 4) circular needles,
40cm (16in) long
2.5mm (UK 12, US C/2) crochet hook

Notions 5 snap fasteners
Stitch holders

Tension (gauge) 24 sts in st st using 3.5mm
(UK 10–9, US 4) needles = 10cm (4in)

Washing Wash the garment in a suitable wool
detergent. After washing, spread it out on a
towel to dry.

Back   Using 3mm (UK 11, US 2–3) circular needle
and yarn A, cast on 18(21:23:25) sts and work in k1,
p1 rib for 5 rows.
Change to 3.5mm (UK 10–9, US 4) circular needle and
cont working in st st, inc 1 st at each end of every
other row a total of ten(eleven:twelve:fourteen) times
and then on every fourth row two(two:three:three)
times (42(47:53:59) sts).
Work 2 rows in st st then place sts on a stitch holder.

Front   Using 3mm (UK 11, US 2–3) circular needle
and yarn A, cast on 18(21:23:25) sts and work in k1, p1
rib for 5 rows.
Change to 3.5mm (UK 10–9, US 4) circular needle and
cont working in st st, inc 1 st at each end of every
fourth row a total of three(four:five:six) times.
Work 2 rows st st.
Cast on 9(9:10:11) sts at each end of next row
(42(47:53:59) sts).

Body   Transfer the sts for the Back onto the needle
with the Front sts and join to work in the round
(84(94:106:118) sts).
Cont in st st until work measures 17(19:21:24)cm /
6¾(7½:8¼:9½)in from where you joined Back
and Front.
Shape armholes as foll: cast off (bind off) 4 sts,
k34(39:45:51), cast off (bind off) 8 sts, k34(39:45:51),
cast off (bind off) 4 sts.
Turn and work on first 34(39:45:51) sts for Back only;
place rem 34(39:45:51) sts on a stitch holder for Front.

Back   Cont in st st, working in rows, until Back
measures 8(9:10:11)cm / 3¼(3½:4:4½)in from armhole.
K8(9:10:12) and then place these sts on a holder, then
cast off (bind off) 18(21:25:27) sts for neck opening.
Change to 3mm (UK 11, US 2–3) circular needle and
work in k1, p1 rib for 5 rows over rem 8(9:10:12) sts for
left shoulder and button band.

Front   Place sts for Front back on needle and rejoin
yarn. Cont in st st, working in rows and foll the chart
to place motif at centre front.
Work 2(3:4:5) rows st st.

Shape neck as foll: work 11(13:16:18) sts in st st, then turn and work on these sts only, casting off (binding off) 1 st at neck edge of every other row three(four:six:six) times (8(9:10:12) sts).
Cont in st st without shaping until work measures same as Back; place sts on a stitch holder.
Rejoin yarn to rem sts and cast off (bind off) 12(13:13:15) sts for neck opening.
Cont on rem 11(13:16:18) sts casting off (binding off) 1 st at neck edge of every other row three(four:six:six) times (8(9:10:12) sts).
Cont in st st without shaping until work measures same as Back.

Shoulders   Bring the Front and Back RS tog at the right shoulder and work a 3-needle cast off (bind off). Using 3mm (UK 11, US 2–3) circular needle, work in k1, p1 rib for 5 rows on left shoulder.

Finishing   Using 2.5mm (UK 12 and US C/2) crochet hook and yarn A, work 1 row of dc around the neck, armhole and leg edges. Change to B and work 1 row crab st (a row of dc worked backwards) round the neck, armhole and leg edges. Add one snap fastener at the left shoulder and four at the crotch.

Chart

BONNET

Difficulty * *

Sizes 3(6-9:12-18) months

Yarn
Navia Uno (50g/1¾oz); in Light Grey (12) and
Pastel Pink (132)

Quantity
A – Light Grey, 1 ball for each size
B – Pastel Pink, 1 ball for each size

Suggested needles 3.5mm (UK 10–9, US 4)
straight needles
3mm (UK11, US C/2–D/3) crochet hook

Notions
1 grey pompom, 3–4cm (1¼–1½in) wide

Tension (gauge) 24 sts in st st using 3.5mm
(UK 10–9, US 4) needles = 10cm (4in)

Washing Wash the garment in a suitable wool
detergent. After washing, spread it out on a
towel to dry.

Using 3.5mm (UK 10–9, US 4) needles and yarn A, cast
on 31(33:35) sts and k 1 row.
Cont in g st, inc and dec on next row as foll: **k3, yrn,
k to last 3 sts, skpo, k1.
Inc and dec in this way on every other row
twelve(fourteen:sixteen) more times.
K 1 row.
Dec and inc on next row as foll: k3, skpo, k to last st,
yrn, k1. Dec and inc in this way on every other row
twelve(fourteen:sixteen) more times.
K 1 row **.
Rep from ** to ** once more, but work only
five(six:seven) inc-and-dec rows (ten(twelve:fourteen)
rows total) and then five(six:seven) dec-and-inc rows
(ten(twelve:fourteen) rows total).
Rep from ** to ** once more
Cast off (bind off).

Finishing Join the sides along one long edge. Sew
the points together at the top.
Using 3mm (UK 11, US C/2–D/3) crochet hook and
two strands of yarn B, crochet two lengths of chain
about 50cm (19¾in) long and attach to either side of
Bonnet for ties.
Sew the pompom to the top of the Bonnet.

BOOTIES

Difficulty * * *

Size 3–6 months

Yarn Navia Uno (50g/1¾oz); in Light Grey (12), Pastel Pink (132) and Mid Grey (13)

Quantity
A – Light Grey, 1 ball for each size
B – Pastel Pink, 1 ball for each size
C – Mid Grey, 1 ball for each size

Suggested needles 3.5mm (UK 10–9, US 4) DPN
3mm (UK 11, US C/2–D/3) crochet hook

Tension (gauge) 24 sts in st st using 3.5mm (UK 10–9, US 4) needles = 10cm (4in)

Note Work is begun under the foot, at the centre.

Washing Wash the garment in a suitable wool detergent. After washing, spread it out on a towel to dry.

Using two 3.5mm (UK 10–9, US 4) DPN and yarn A, cast on 56 sts.
K 20 rows.
K24; leave these sts on right-hand needle for one side of the foot, then, using another DPN, k8 (for centre of foot). Leave the rem 24 sts on left-hand needle for other side of foot, then **turn work and, using another DPN, k across the centre-foot sts, working last st of centre-foot tog with first st of side of foot. Rep from ** until 15 sts rem on each side of foot, k to end.
Working across all 38 sts, k 8 rows.
Eyelet row: *k3, (yo) twice, k3tog, rep from * to last 2 sts, k2.
K 1 row, dec by 1 st (37 sts).
P 1 row, then work in st st and foll chart to work design on cuff.
Work 4 rows g st.
Cast off (bind off) loosely.
Make another bootee the same way.
Sew together under the foot and centre back.

Finishing Using 3mm (UK 11, US C/2–D/3) crochet hook and two strands of yarn B, crochet two lengths of chain about 50cm (19¾in) long for ties. Thread a tie through the eyelets on each bootee.

Chart

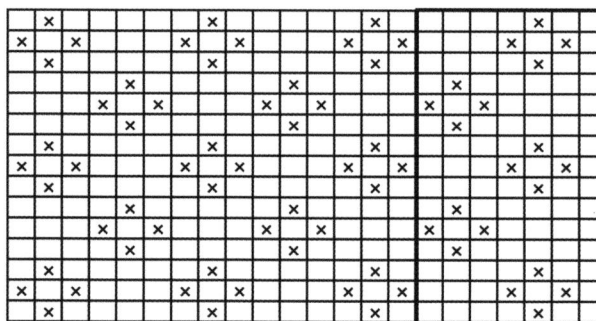

Repeat

☐ A   ⊠ C

BABY BLANKET

Difficulty * * *

Size approx. 80 x 90cm (32 x 36in)

Yarn Navia Uno (50g/1¾oz); in White (11)

Quantity 4 balls

Suggested needles 3.5mm (UK 10–9, US 4) circular needles, 60 or 80cm (24 or 32in) long

Tension (gauge) 27 sts over pattern using 3.5mm (UK 10–9, US 4) needles = 10cm (4in)

Washing Wash the garment in a suitable wool detergent. After washing, spread it out on a towel to dry.

Using 3.5mm (UK 10–9, US 4) circular needle, cast on 215 sts.
K 8 rows.
Row 1 (RS): k5, work the 34 sts of chart six times, then work first st of chart, k5.
Row 2 (WS): k5, work first st of chart, then work the 34 sts of chart six times, k5.
These 2 rows set the position of the charted design with g st borders. Rep until the work measures 89cm (35in) ending on a final row of the chart.
K 8 rows.
Cast off (bind off).

Chart

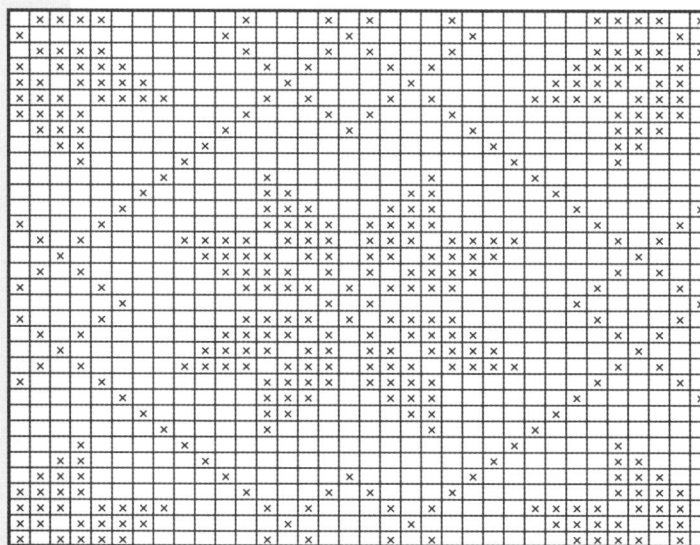

↑
Start pattern here

☐ k on right side, p on wrong side

☒ p on right side, k on wrong side

STAR-PATTERNED SHORT-SLEEVED SWEATER

pattern: model 4 – NB56 (on www.navia.fo)

design: Sára Mrdalo

STAR-PATTERNED
SHORT-SLEEVED SWEATER

Difficulty * * * *

Sizes XS/S(M:L:XL:XXL)

Bust 81(93:105:117:130)cm / 32(36½:41¼:46:51¼)in

Length 47(52:57:62:67)cm / 18½(20½:22½:24½:26½)in

Yarn Navia Uno (50g/1¾oz); in Bottle Green (113) and White (11)

Quantity
A – Bottle Green, 2(3:4:5:6) balls
B – White, 1(2:3:4:5) balls

Suggested needles 2.5mm and 3.5mm (UK 13–12 and 10–9, US 1–2 and 4) circular needles, 60 or 80cm (24 or 32in long) 3.5mm (UK 10–9, US 4) straight needles 2.5mm and 3.5mm (UK 13–12 and 10–9, US 1–2 and 4) DPN

Notions Stitch holders

Tension (gauge) 26 sts over pattern using 3.5mm (UK 10–9, US 4) needles = 10cm (4in)

Washing Wash the garment in a suitable wool detergent. After washing, spread it out on a towel to dry.

Back and Front   Using 2.5mm (UK 13–12, US 1-2) circular needle and yarn A, cast on 210(242:274:306:338) sts and join to work in the round. Work in k1, p1 rib for 12 rounds.
Change to 3.5mm (UK 10–9, US 4) circular needle and cont in st st, working from the charts: k1 in yarn A, k103(119:135:151:167) from Front chart, k2 in yarn A, k103(119:135:151:167) from Back chart, k1 in yarn A. Cont working rounds in this way until work measures 29(31:33:35:37)cm / 11½(12¼:13:13¾:14½)in.
While maintaining pattern, divide for Back and Front as foll: cast off (bind off) 5 sts, k95(111:127:143:159), cast off (bind off) 10 sts, k95(111:127:143:159), cast off (bind off) 5 sts.
Turn and cont on first 95(111:127:143:159) sts for Back; place rem 95(111:127:143:159) sts (for Front) on a stitch holder.

Back   While maintaining pattern, cont in st st, working in rows, and shape armholes as foll: cast off (bind off) 1 st at each end of every other row until 83(95:107:119:131) sts rem.**
While maintaining pattern, cont in st st without shaping until Back measures 46(49:52:56:61cm / 18(19¼:20½:22:24)in, ending on a WS row.
Shape neck as foll: k20(23:27:32:37), turn and work on these sts only for left side of neck.
At same time as working in st st and foll chart, cast off (bind off) 1(1:1:2:2) sts at beg of next row, then 1 st at beg of foll alt row(s) until 18(20:24:28:33) sts rem. Place these sts on a holder.
With RS facing, rejoin yarn and cast off (bind off) next 43(49:53:(55:57) sts. Work rem 20(23:27:32:37) sts in st st, foll chart, and at same time work dec at neck edge as for right side of neck. Leave sts on a holder.

Front   Place sts for Front back on needles and rejoin yarn; work as for Back to **.
While maintaining pattern, cont in st st without shaping until Front measures 39(42:45:49:54)cm / 15¼(16½:17¾:19¼:21¼)in, ending on a WS row.
Shape neck as foll: k27(31:36:42:47), turn and work on these sts only for left side of neck.
Working in st st and foll chart, at same time cast off (bind off) 1 st at neck edge on every other row until 18(20:24:28:33) sts rem.
Cont without shaping until left side of Front measures the same as Back, ending on a RS row. Cut yarn and place sts on a stitch holder.

With RS facing, rejoin yarn and cast off (bind off) next 29(33:35:35:37) sts. Work rem 27(31:36:42:47)sts in st st, foll chart, and at the same time work dec at neck edge as for left side of neck.

Cont without shaping until right side of Front measures the same as Back, ending on a RS row. Transfer sts for the Back to a 3.5mm (UK 10–9, US 4) straight needle, then hold Back and right-hand side of Front RS tog and work a 3-needle cast off (bind off) until all the sts of the Front have been cast off (bound off). Use the same technique to join the left-hand side of Front and Back tog.

Sleeve (make 2) Using 2.5mm (UK 13–12, US 1–2) DPN and yarn A, cast on 50(60:72:84:96) sts and join to work in the round. Work in k1, p1 rib for 12 rounds. Change to 3.5mm (UK 10–9, US 4) DPN and k 1 round, inc evenly by 28(30:30:28:28) sts over the round (78(90:102:112:124) sts).

Cont in st st and foll Sleeve chart until work measures 4(5:6:7:8)cm / 1½(2:2¼:2¾:3¼)in.

Cast off (bind off) 5 sts at beg and end of next round, then cont on rem 68(80:92:102:114) sts, foll chart and now working in rows in st st, shape Sleeve cap as foll: cast off (bind off) 1 st at each end of every sixth row six(seven:eight:nine:ten) times (56(66:76:84:94) sts). Work without further shaping until the sleeve measures 23(25:28:31:34)cm / 9(9¾:11:12¼:13½)in. Cast off (bind off).

Neckband Using 2.5mm (UK 13–12, US 1–2) circular needle and yarn A, pick up and k 126(138:148:158:168) sts around the neck. Work in k1, p1 rib for 12 rounds. Cast off (bind off) in rib.

Finishing Fold the centre top of each sleeve into a pleat about 3(3.5:4:4.5:5)cm / 1¼(1½:1½:1¾:2)in deep so that the sleeve fits into the armhole. Pin the pleats in place and sew in the sleeves.

Front chart

Back/Sleeves chart

☐ A

[x] B

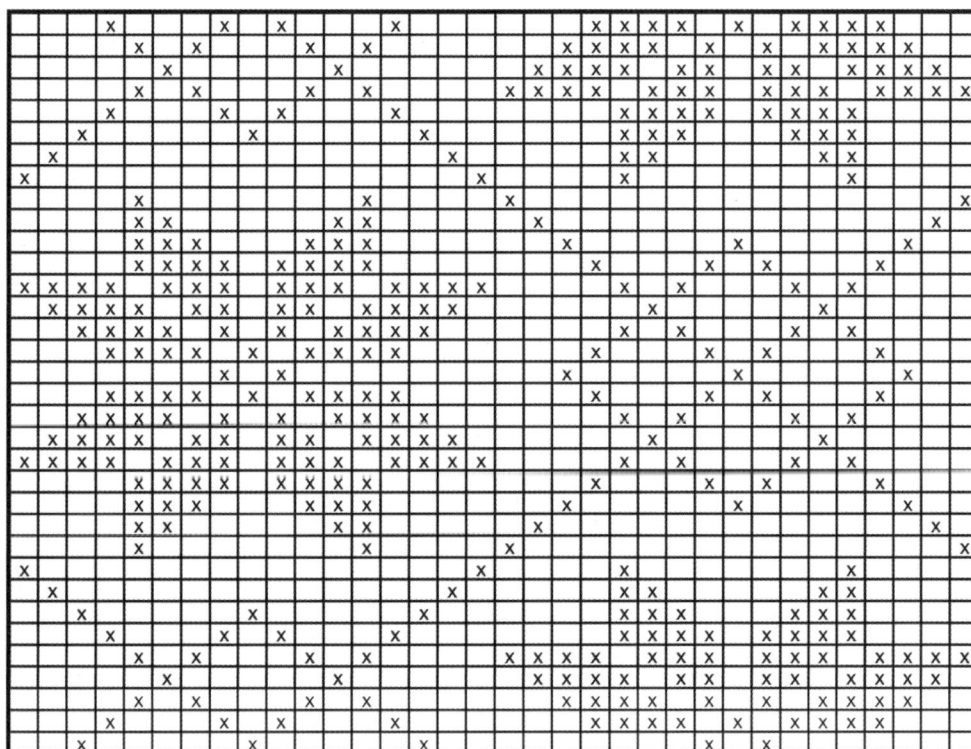

Start here for size L

Start here for size XXL

Start here for size XL

Start here for size XS/S

Start here for size M

PATTERNED SWEATER

pattern: model 1 – NB44 (on www.navia.fo)
design: Gunnvør Frederiksberg

PATTERNED SWEATER

Difficulty * *

Sizes S(M:L)

Chest/bust 100(110:120)cm / 39¼(43¼:47¼)in

Length 65(71:76)cm / 25½(28:30)in

Yarn Navia Tradition (50g/1¾oz); in Dark Brown (906), White (901) and Mid Grey (903)

Quantity
A – Dark brown, 8(10:12) balls
B – White, 2 balls for each size
C – Mid Grey, 4(6:6) balls

Suggested needles 6mm and 7mm (UK 4 and 2, US 10 and 10½–11) circular needles, 60cm (24in) long
7mm (UK 2, US 10½–11) straight needles
6mm and 7mm (UK 4 and 2, US 10 and 10½–11) DPN or circular needle, 40cm (16in) long

Notions Stitch holders

Tension (gauge) 16 sts over st st using 7mm (UK 2, US 10½–11) needles = 10cm (4in)

Washing Wash the garment in a suitable wool detergent. After washing, spread it out on a towel to dry.

Back and Front   Using 6mm (UK 4 and US 10) circular needle and yarn A, 60cm (24in) long, cast on 160(176:192) sts and join to work in the round. Work in k1, p1 rib for 8cm (3¼in).
Change to 7mm (UK 2, US 10½–11) circular needle, 60cm (24in) long, and cont in st st, foll the chart, until work measures 45:(50:54)cm / 17¾(19¾:21¼)in. While maintaining chart pattern, divide for Back and Front as foll: cast off (bind off) 6 sts, k69(77:85), cast off (bind off) 11 sts, k69(77:85), cast off (bind off) 5 sts. Turn and cont on first 69(77:85) sts for Back; place rem 69(77:85) sts (for Front) on a stitch holder.

Back   Cont in st st and foll chart, work in rows without shaping until Back measures 65(71:76)cm / 25½(28:30)in. Place sts on a stitch holder.

Front   Place sts for Front back on needles and rejoin yarn. Cont in st st and foll chart, work in rows without shaping until Front measures 58(63:67)cm)/22¾:24¾:26½)in, ending on a WS row. Shape neck as foll: k27(30:33), turn and work on these sts only for left side of neck.
At same time as working in st st and foll chart, cast off (bind off) 2 sts at beg of next row, 1(2:2) st(s) at beg of foll alt row and 1 st at beg of foll alt row once(once:twice) (23(25:27) sts).
Cont without shaping until left side of Front measures the same as Back, ending on a RS row. Cut yarn and place sts on a stitch holder.
With RS facing, rejoin yarn and cast off (bind off) next 15(17:19) sts.
Continue on rem 27(30:33) sts and work dec at neck edge as for left side of neck, and at same time work in st st and foll chart.
Cont without shaping until right side of Front measures the same as Back, ending on a RS row. Transfer the sts for the Back to a 7mm (UK 2, US 10½–11) straight needle, then hold Back and right-hand side of Front RS tog and work a 3-needle cast off (bind off) until all the sts of the Front have been cast off (bound off). Use the same technique to join the left-hand side of Front and Back tog.

Sleeves (make 2)   Using 6mm (UK 4 and US 10) DPN or circular needle 40cm (16in) long and yarn A, cast on 40(42:44) sts and join to work in the round. Work in k1, p1 rib for 8cm (3¼in).

Change to 7mm (UK 2, US 10½–11) DPN or circular needle, 40cm (16in) long, and cont in st st, inc by 1 st on first round (41(43:45 sts).

Cont in st st, foll chart, and at same time inc 1 st at both beg and end of every fourth round until there are 71(77:83) sts.

Cont in st st, foll chart and without shaping until sleeve measures 55(57:58)cm / 21¾(22½:22¾)in.
Cast off (bind off).

Neckband   Using 6mm (UK 4 and US 10) circular needle and yarn A, 60cm (24in) long, pick up and k about 80(86:92) sts around the neck (make sure you have an even number).
Work in k1, p1 rib for 9cm (3½in).
Cast off (bind off) loosely in rib.

Finishing   Turn under the edge of the neckband and sew loosely in place. Sew in the sleeves.

Chart

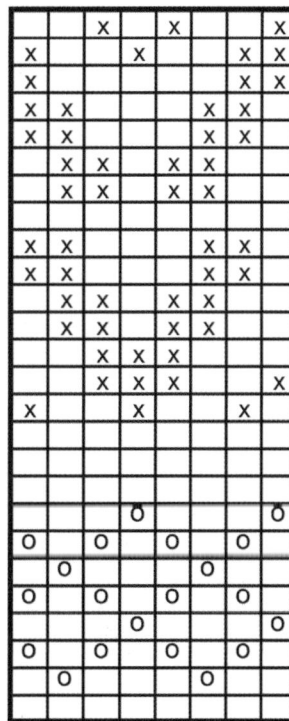

Key:
- A
- B (○)
- C (x)

Start here for Sleeve size M

Start here for Sleeve size L

Start here for Front/Back for all sizes and for Sleeve size S

HIGH-NECK SWEATER WITH ALL-OVER PATTERN

pattern: model 4 – NB44 (on www.navia.fo)

design: Oddvör Jacobsen

HIGH-NECK SWEATER WITH ALL-OVER PATTERN

Difficulty * * *

Sizes XS/S(S/M:L)

Chest/bust 84(96:108)cm / 33(37¾:42½)in

Length 58(63:67)cm / 22¾(24¾:26½)in

Yarn Navia Brushed Tradition (50g/1¾oz); in Off-white (1101), Light Brown (1105) and Dark Brown (1106)

Quantity
A – Off-white, 6(6:8) balls
B – Light Brown, 2 balls for each size
C – Dark Brown, 4(4:6) balls

Suggested needles 4mm (UK 8, US 6) circular needles, 40cm and 60cm (16 and 24in) long
5mm (UK 6, US 8) circular needles, 40cm and 80cm (16 and 32in) long
4mm and 5mm (UK 8 and 6, US 6 and 8) DPN

Notions Stitch markers
Stitch holders

Tension (gauge) 20 sts over pattern using 5mm (UK 6, US 8) needles = 10cm (4in)

Washing Wash the garment in a suitable wool detergent. After washing, spread it out on a towel to dry.

Back and Front   Using 4mm (UK 8, US 6) circular needle and yarn A, 60cm (24in) long, cast on 168(192:216) sts and join to work in the round. Work in k2, p2 rib for 12 rounds.
Change to 5mm (UK 6, US 8) circular needle, 60cm (24in) long, and cont in st st, foll the chart, until work measures 36(40:43)cm / 14¼(15¾:17)in.
While maintaining chart pattern, divide for Back and Front as foll: cast off (bind off) 4 sts, k77(89:101), cast off (bind off) 7 sts, k77(89:101), cast off (bind off) 3 sts. Leave work on needle.

Sleeves (make 2)   Using 4mm (UK 8, US 6) DPN and yarn A, cast on 40(42:44) sts and join to work in the round. Work in k2, p2 rib for 12 rounds.
Change to 5mm (UK 6, US 8) DPN and k 1 round, inc evenly by 8(8:10) sts over the round (48(50:54) sts.
Cont in st st, foll chart, and at same time inc 1 st and both beg and end of every tenth(twelfth:ninth) round until you have 66(72:78) sts.
Shape underarms as foll: cast off (bind off) 4 sts, k59(65:71), cast off (bind off) 3 sts (59(65:71) sts).
Note the pattern on the sleeve must end at same point as pattern on Back and Front.
Place sts on a stitch holder.

Raglan shaping   Arrange the sts of Back, Front and Sleeves on the 5mm (UK 6, US 8) circular needle, 80cm (32in) long, as foll: 77(89:101) sts for Front, PM, 59(65:71) sts for a Sleeve, PM, 77(89:101) sts for Back, PM, 59(65:71) sts for another Sleeve, PM (272(308:344) sts).
Rejoin yarn to beg first round between left Sleeve and Front and work 4 rounds in st st, foll chart.
Sizes XS/S and L only
Maintaining pattern and cont in st st, dec for raglan shaping as folls:
Next round: (k2tog, k to 2 sts before M, skpo) four times.
Next round: k to end.
Rep these 2 rounds until 128(–:136) sts rem.
Size S/M only
Maintaining pattern and cont in st st, dec for raglan shaping on every other row as folls:
Next round: (k to M, sl M, k2tog, k to 2 sts before M, skpo) twice.
Next round: k to end.
Rep these 2 rounds once more (-(300:-) sts).
Then dec as folls:

Next round: (k2tog, k to 2 sts before M, skpo) four times.
Next round: k to end.
Rep these 2 rounds until -(132:-) sts rem.

All sizes
Shape the neck as foll: cut yarn, then reorganize sts so centre 15(17:19) sts of Front are on a stitch holder and you are beg to work, with RS facing, to the right of these centre sts.
Commence working in st st in rows, maintaining pattern and at same time dec for raglan shaping on RS rows.
Cast off (bind off) 3 sts at beg of next 2 rows (99(101:103) sts).
Cast off (bind off) 2(2:3) sts at beg of next 2 rows (87(89:89) sts).

Cast off (bind off) 1(2:2) sts at both beg and end of next row (77(77:77) sts.)
Cut off the yarn.

Neckband Transfer sts to the shorter 4mm (UK 8 and US 6) circular needle; using A pick up and k 4(5:8) sts along neck edge, k the 15(17:19) sts on stitch holder for centre Front, pick up and k 4(5:8) sts on other neck edge (100(104:112) sts).
Join to work in the round, and work in k2, p2 rib for 30 rounds or to desired length.

Finishing Sew together at the underarms.

Chart

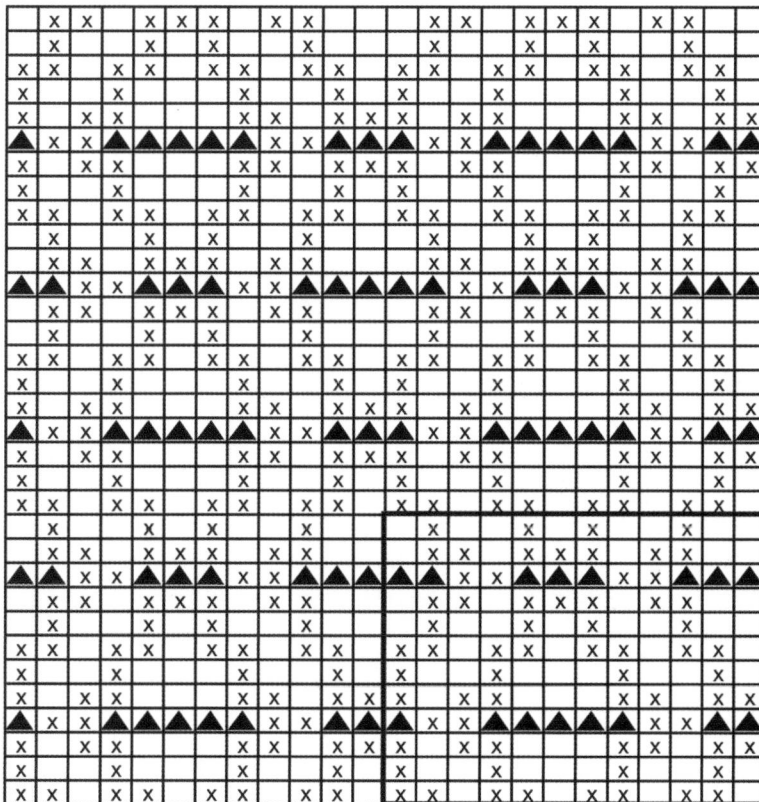

A

B

C

Repeat

↑
Start here for Sleeve for size L

Start here for Back and Front for all sizes
and for Sleeve for sizes XS/S and S/M

CHILD'S SWEATER

påttern: model 21 – NB27 (on www.navia.fo)
design: Harriet Jørginsdóttir

CHILD'S SWEATER

Difficulty * *

Sizes 6(8:10) years

Chest 68(76:84)cm / 26¾(30:33)in

Length 44(49:54)cm / 17¼(19¼:21¼)in

Yarn Navia Duo (50g/1¾oz); in Denim Blue (239), Light Grey (22)

Quantity
A – Denim Blue, 4(4:5) balls
B – Light Grey, 1 ball for each size

Suggested needles 3mm and 4mm (UK 11 and 8, US 2–3 and 6) circular needles, 60 or 80cm (24 or 32in) long
4mm straight needles (UK 8, US 6)
3mm and 4mm (UK 11 and 8, US 2–3 and 6) DPN

Notions Stitch holders

Tension (gauge) 21 sts in st st using 4mm (UK 8, US 6) needles = 10cm (4in)

Washing Wash the garment in a suitable wool detergent. After washing, spread it out on a towel to dry.

Back and Front Using 3mm (UK 11, US 2–3) circular needle and yarn A, cast on 140(150:160) sts and join to work in the round. Work in k1, p1 rib for 6 rounds. Change to 4mm (UK 8, US 6) circular needle and k 1 round, inc evenly by 4(10:16) sts over the round (144(160:176) sts).
Cont in st st until work measures 25(29:33)cm / 9¾(11½:13)in. Beg working from chart and cont in st st until work measures 31(35:39)cm / 12¼(13¾:15¼)in.
While maintaining chart pattern, divide for Back and Front as foll: cast off (bind off) 5 sts, k62(70:78), cast off 10 sts, k62(70:78)sts, cast off 5 sts.
Turn and cont on first 62(70:78) sts for Back; place rem 62(70:78) sts (for Front) on a stitch holder.

Back While maintaining pattern, cont in st st, working in rows, and shape armholes as foll: cast off (bind off) 1(1:2) sts at each end of next row, then 1 st at each end of every other row until 54(60:66) sts rem.**
While maintaining pattern, cont in st st without shaping until Back measures 44(49:54)cm / 17¼(19¼:21¼)in.
Place the sts on a stitch holder.

Front Place sts for Front back on needles and rejoin yarn; work as for Back to **.
While maintaining pattern, cont in st st without shaping until Front measures 29(34:39)cm / 11½(13½:15¼)in, ending on a WS row.
Shape neck as foll: k16(18:20), turn and work on these sts only for left side of neck.
At same time as working in st st, cast off (bind off) 1 st at beg of next and every foll alt row until 14(14:16) sts rem.
Cont without shaping until left side of Front measures the same as Back, ending on a RS row. Cut yarn and place sts on a stitch holder.
Place centre 22(24:26) sts on a stitch holder. Rejoin yarn to rem 16(18:20) sts and work dec at neck edge as for left side of neck. Cont without shaping until right side of Front measures same as Back.
Transfer the sts for the Back to a 4mm (UK 8, US 6) straight needle, then hold Back and right-hand side of Front RS tog and work a 3-needle cast off (bind off) until all the sts of the Front have been cast off (bound off). Use the same technique to join the left-hand side of Front and Back tog.
Leave rem sts for Back on a stitch holder.

Chart

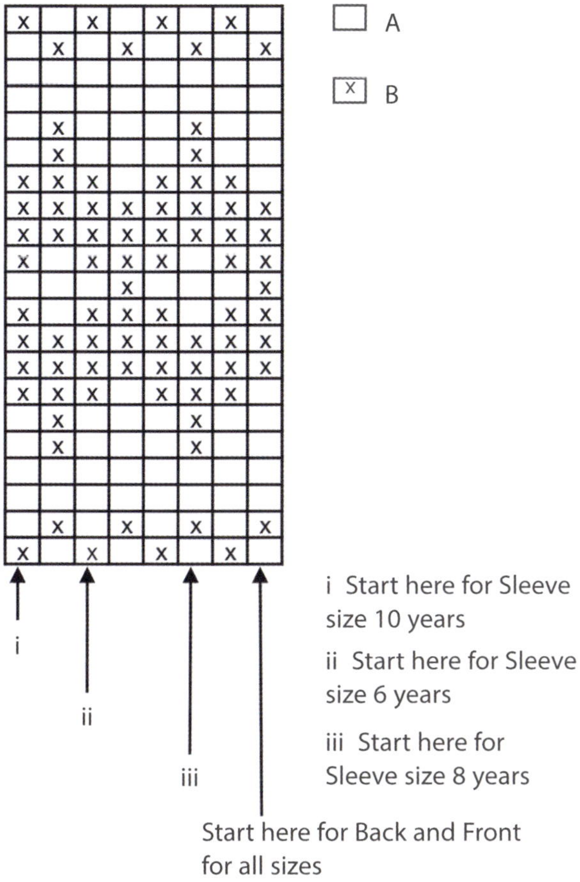

□ A

▣ B

i Start here for Sleeve size 10 years

ii Start here for Sleeve size 6 years

iii Start here for Sleeve size 8 years

Start here for Back and Front for all sizes

Sleeves (make 2) Using A and 3mm (UK 11 and US 2–3) DPN, cast on 34(36:38) sts and join to work in the round. Work in k1, p1 rib for 6 rounds.
Change to 4mm (UK 8 and US 6) DPN and k 1 round, inc evenly by 7(9:11) sts over the round (41(45:49) sts). Cont in st st, inc by 1 st at both beg and end or every seventh round until you have 55(61:67) sts. At the same time, when the sleeve measures 28(33:38)cm / 11(13:15)in, work the pattern from the chart until you have reached the same point in the pattern as where you divided the Back and Front.
Cast off (bind off) 5 sts each at end of the round and beg of foll round, then cont on rem 45(51:57) sts, foll chart and now working in rows in st st, shape sleeve cap as foll: cast off (bind off) 1 st at beg of every row until 28(30:34) sts rem, then cast off (bind off) 1 st at the beg and end of every row until 10(12:12) sts rem. Cast off (bind off).

Neckband Using 3mm (UK 11 and US 2–3) circular needle and yarn A, starting at the left shoulder, pick up and k 14(12:12) sts along the neck edge, k the 22(24:26) sts on the stitch holder for centre Front, pick up and k 14(12:12) sts along the neck edge, k the 26(32:34) sts on the stitch holder for the Back neck (76(80:84)sts). Work in k1, p1 rib for 11 rounds. Cast off (bind off) in rib.

Finishing Sew in the sleeves.

WHITE UNISEX SWEATER

pattern: model 1 – NB27 (on www.navia.fo)

design: Malan Steinhólm

WHITE UNISEX SWEATER

Difficulty * * * *

Sizes S(M:L)

Chest/bust 81(93:104)cm / 32(36½:41)in

Length 63(68:73)cm / 24¾(26¾:28¾)in

Yarn Navia Trio (50g/1¾oz); in White (31)

Quantity 9(9:11) balls

Suggested needles 3.5mm and 6mm
(UK 10–9 and 4, US 4 and 10) circular needles,
80cm (32in) long
3.5mm and 6mm (UK 10–9 and 4,
US 4 and 10) DPN
Cable needle

Notions Stitch holders

Tension (gauge) 19 sts over pattern using
6mm (UK 4, US 10) needles = 10cm (4in)

Special abbreviations:
C4B = slip next 2 sts onto cable needle, leave
at back of work, k2, then k2 from cable needle.
C4F = slip next 2 sts onto cable needle, leave
at front of work, k2, then k2 from cable needle.

Washing Wash the garment in a suitable wool
detergent. After washing, spread it out on a
towel to dry.

Pattern 1: (worked in rounds)
Rounds 1–4: *p3, k8, rep from * to end of round.
Round 5: *p3, C4B, C4F, rep from * to end of round.
Round 6: *p3, k8, rep from * to end of round.
Rep these six rounds.
Pattern 2: (worked in rows)
Row 1 (RS): *p3, k8, rep from * to end of row.
Row 2: *k3, p8, rep from * to end of row.
Row 3: *p3, k8, rep from * to end of row.
Row 4: *k3, p8, rep from * to end of row.
Row 5: *p3, C4B, C4F, rep from * to end of row.
Row 6: *k3, p8, rep from * to end of row.
Rep these six rows.
Pattern 3: (worked in rounds)
Round 1 and all odd-numbered rounds: k to end
of round.
Round 2 and all even-numbered rounds: *p1, ytb, sl1
purl-wise, ytf, rep from * to end of round.
Pattern 4: (worked in rows)
Row 1 and all odd-numbered rows (WS): p to
end row.
Row 2 and all even-numbered rows: *p1, ytb, sl1
purlwise, ytf *, rep from * to end or row.

Back and Front   Using 3.5mm (UK 10–9, US 4)
circular needle, cast on 138(160:182)sts and join to
work in the round. Work in k1, p1 rib for 6cm (2¼in).
Change to 6mm (UK 4, US 10) circular needle and
work in Pattern 1, inc evenly by 16 sts over first round
(154(176:198) sts).
Cont in pattern without shaping until work measures
40(44:48)cm / 15¾(17¼:19)in, finishing with a
Round 6 of pattern.
Divide for Back and Front as foll: cast off (bind off)
5 sts, work 70(81:92) sts in Pattern 2, cast off (bind off)
7 sts, work 70(81:92) sts in Pattern 2, cast off (bind off)
2 sts.
Turn and cont on first 70(81:92) sts for Back; place rem
70(81:92) sts (for Front) on a stitch holder.

Back   Cont in Pattern 2 and working in rows, shape
armholes as foll: cast off (bind off) 2(1:1) sts at each
end on every other row until 62(73:84) sts rem.**
Continue in Pattern 2 without shaping until work
measures 16(17:18)cm / 6¼(6¾:7)in from beg of
armhole. Cast off (bind off) 4 sts at beg of every row
until 22(25:28) sts rem. Place sts on a stitch holder.

Front   Place sts for Front back on needles and rejoin yarn; work as for Back to **.

Continue in Pattern 2 without shaping until work measures 13(14:15)cm / 5(5½:6)in from beg of armhole, ending on a WS row.

Shape neck and shoulders as foll: k25(29:33), turn and work on these sts only for left side of neck.

At same time as working in Pattern 2, *cast off (bind off) 2 sts at the neck edge and 4 sts at armhole edge on next row. Rep from * once. Cast off (bind off) 5 sts at armhole edge on next alt row. Cast off (bind off) 1 st at the neck edge and 4 sts at armhole edge on next row.

Size S only

Fasten off.

Size M only

Cast off (bind off) 4 sts at armhole edge on next alt row.

Fasten off.

Size L only

Cast off (bind off) 4 sts at armhole edge on next alt row twice.

Fasten off.

All sizes

Place centre 12(15:18) sts on a stitch holder. Rejoin yarn to rem 25(29:33) sts and work dec as for left side of neck.

Sleeves (make 2)   Using 3.5mm (UK 10–9, US 4) DPN, cast on 36(36:38) sts and join to work in the round. Work in k1, p1 rib for 6cm (2¼in).

Change to 6mm (UK 4, US 10) circular needle and cont in Pattern 3, inc by 1 st at both beg and end of every eleventh round until you have 50(56:62) sts. Continue without shaping until the sleeve measures 45(50:50)cm / 17¾(19¾:19¾)in.

Cast off (bind off) 3 sts each at end of the round and beg of foll round, then cont on rem 44(50:56) sts, working in rows from Pattern 4 as foll: cast off (bind off) 2 sts at beg of next row, then 1 st at beg of every other row until 20(24:28) sts rem.

Cont working in Pattern 4 until you have a strip the same length as the cast-off (bound-off) edge of the shoulders on Back and Front.

Place sts on a stitch holder.

Neckband   Pick up and k sts down left front neck edge, pick up sts for Front from stitch holder, pick up and k sts up right front neck (making sure you have same amount as left front neck), pick up sts from a Sleeve, from Back and rem Sleeve. Join to work in the round. K 1 round, dec evenly to 82(88:94) sts. Work in k1, p1 rib for 9cm (3½in). Cast off (bind off) in rib.

Finishing   Sew in the sleeves, joining the straight strip to shoulder edges of Front and Back.

SWEATER WITH CIRCULAR YOKE

pattern: model 2 – NB44 (on www.navia.fo)

design: Tóra Joensen

SWEATER WITH CIRCULAR YOKE

Difficulty * *

Sizes S(M:L)

Chest/bust 94(103:111)cm / 37(40½:43¾)in

Length 59(64:67)cm / 23¼(25¼:26½)in

Yarn Navia Tradition (50g/1¾oz); in Light Brown (905), Dark Brown (906) and White (901)

Quantity
A – Light Brown, 2(4:4) balls
B – Dark Brown, 2 balls for each size
C – White, 8(10:12) balls

Suggested needles 5mm and 5.5m (UK 6 and 5, US 8 and 9) circular needles, 60cm (24in) long
5mm (UK 6, US 8) circular needle, 40cm (16in) long
5mm and 5.5mm (UK 6 and 5, US 8 and 9) DPN

Notions Stitch holders

Tension (gauge) 14 sts in st st using 5.5mm (UK 5, US 9) needles = 10cm (4in)

Washing Wash the garment in a suitable wool detergent. After washing, spread it out on a towel to dry.

Back and Front   Using 5mm (UK 6, US 8) circular needle, 60cm (24in) long, and yarn A, cast on 132(144:156) sts and join to work in the round. Work in k1, p1 rib for 5cm (2in).
Change to 5.5mm (UK 5, US 9) circular needle and work 10(12:14) rounds in st st. Then work the pattern from chart 1.
Cont in st st in yarn C until work measures 38(42:44) cm / 15(16½:17¼)in.
Divide for Back and Front as follows: cast off (bind off) 5 sts, k56(62:68), cast off (bind off) 10 sts, k56(62:68) sts, cast off (bind off) 5 sts. Cut yarn and leave the work on the needle.

Sleeves (make 2)   Using 5mm (UK 6, US 8) DPN and yarn A cast on 34(36:38) sts and join to work in the round. Work in k1, p1 rib for 5cm (2in).
Change to 5.5mm (UK 5, US 9) DPN and k 1 round, inc evenly by 2(4:6) sts over the round (36(40:44) sts).
Work 9(11:13) rounds in st st, then work pattern from Chart 1, then in st st in yarn C, and at the same time, inc by 1 st at both beg and end of every fifth round until you have 50(56:62) sts.
Cont in st st without shaping until sleeve measures 44(48:48)cm / 17¼(19:19)in.
Cast off (bind off) 5 sts at beg and end of next round (40(46:52) sts).
Leave sts on a stitch holder.

Yoke   Arrange the sts on the 5.5mm (UK 5, US 9) circular needle so you have the sts for Front, for a Sleeve, for Back and for other Sleeve tog on the needle (192(216:240) sts).
Join to work in the round and work in st st for 4(8:12) rounds in yarn C without shaping. Then work the pattern and dec from chart 2; you should end up with 112(126:140) sts on the needle.
K 1 round, dec by 34(40:48) sts evenly over the round (78(86:92) sts).
Change to 5mm (UK 6, US 8) circular needle, 40cm (16in) long, and k 1 round, dec by 18(24:24) evenly over the round (60(62:68) sts).

Neckband   Cont in k1, p1 rib until Neckband measures 20cm (8in).
Cast off (bind off) in rib.

Finishing   Sew together at the underarms.

Legend

Symbol	Meaning
▲	A
×	B
☐	C
◢▲	k2tog in A
✕×	k2tog in B

Chart 1

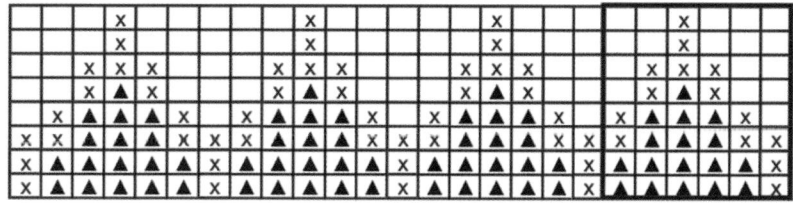

Repeat

Start here for Sleeve size M

Start here for Sleeve size L

Start here for Sleeve size S

Chart 2

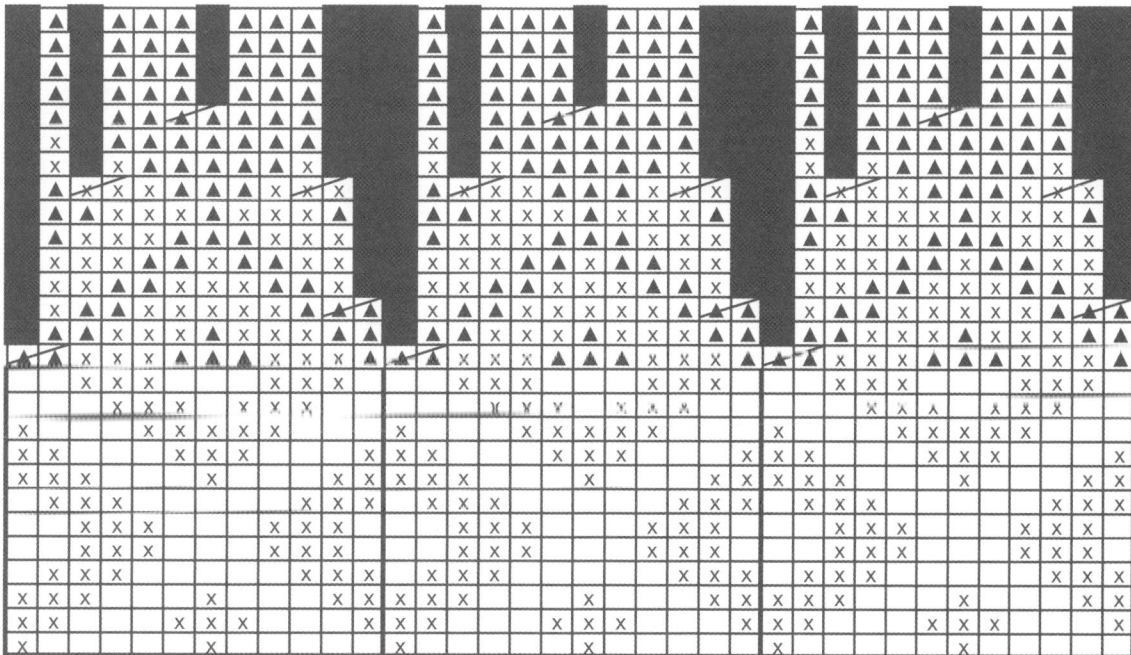

Start here for all sizes

127

RAGLAN SWEATER

pattern: model 3 – NB58 (on www.navia.fo)
design: Gunnvør Frederiksberg

RAGLAN SWEATER

Difficulty * * *

Sizes S(S/M:M/L:L/XL)

Chest/bust 94(99:104:110)cm / 37(39:41:43¼)in

Length 66(70:73:76)cm / 26(27½:28¾:30)in

Yarn Navia Duo (50g/1¾oz); in Charcoal (24), Light Grey (22) and Mid Grey (23)

Quantity
A – Charcoal, 5(6:7:8) balls
B – Light Grey, 2 balls for each size
C – Mid Grey, 1 ball for each size

Suggested needles 3.5mm and 4mm (UK 10–9 and 8, US 4 and 6) circular needles, 60 or 80cm (24 or 32in) long
3.5mm and 4mm (UK 10–9 and 8, US 4 and 6) DPN or shorter circular needles

Notions Stitch holders
Stitch markers

Tension (gauge) 23 sts in st st using 4mm (UK 8, US 6) needles = 10cm (4in)

Washing Wash the garment in a suitable wool detergent. After washing, spread it out on a towel to dry.

Back and Front Using 3.5mm (UK 10–9, US 4) circular needle and yarn A, cast on 216(228:240:252) sts and join to work in the round. Work in k1, p1 rib for 4cm (1½in).
Change to 4mm (UK 8, UK 6) circular needle and work in st st until work measures 42(45:47:49)cm / 16½(17¾:18½:19¼)in.
Divide for Back and Front as foll: cast off (bind off) 4 sts, k101(107:113:119), cast off (bind off) 7 sts, k101(107:113:119), cast off (bind off) 3 sts.
Cut yarn and leave the sts on stitch holders.

Sleeves (make 2) Using 3.5mm (UK 10–9, US 4) DPN and yarn A, cast on 56(58:60:62) sts and join to work in the round. Work in k1, p1 rib for 4cm (1½in).
Change to 4mm (UK 8, UK 6) DPN and work in st st, inc by 1 st at both beg and end of a round every 5(5:4:3)cm / 2(2:1½:1¼)in until you have 72(78:84:90) sts.
Cont without shaping until sleeve measures 50(52:54:55)cm / 19¾:20½:21¼:21¾)in.
Cast off (bind off) 3 sts at beg of next round and 4 sts at end (65(71:77:83) sts).
Leave sts on a stitch holder.

Raglan shaping Arrange the sts of Back, Front and Sleeves on the 4mm (UK 8, UK 6) circular needle as foll: 101(107:113:119) sts for Front, PM, 65(71:77:83) sts sts for a Sleeve, PM, 101(107:113:119) sts for Back, PM, 65(71:77:83) sts sts for another Sleeve, PM, (332(356:380:404) sts).
Rejoin yarn A, beg first round between left Sleeve and Front and k 5(7:9:11) rounds.
Work chart, dec for raglan shaping as folls:
Next round: (k2tog tbl, k1, k from chart to 3 sts before M, k1, k2tog) four times.
Next round: k to end.
When chart is completed, cont in yarn B and dec for raglan shaping as folls:
Next round: (k2tog tbl, k to 2 sts before M, k2tog) four times.
Next round: k to end.
Rep these 2 rounds until 140(148:156:164) sts rem.

Shape neck as foll: k2tog tbl, k15, cast off (bind off) 19(21:23:25) sts, k to 2 sts before M, k2tog; (k2tog tbl, k to 2 sts before M, k2tog) three times (113(119:125:131) sts).
Turn and p 1 row (WS).
Maintaining raglan dec on RS rows, cont in st st and working in rows, cast off (bind off) 2(2:2:3) sts at beg of next two rows; cast off (bind off) 2 sts at beg of next four rows; cast off (bind off) 1(2:2:2) st(s) at beg of next two rows (67(71:77:81) sts).
P 1 row.

Neckband Change to 3.5mm (UK 10–9, US 4) DPN and, cont in yarn B, pick up and k 47 sts around the neck edge (114(118:124:128) sts).
Work in k1, p1 rib for 6cm (2¼in). Cast off (bind off) loosely in rib.

Finishing Turn the neckband under and sew loosely in place. Sew together at the underarms.

Chart

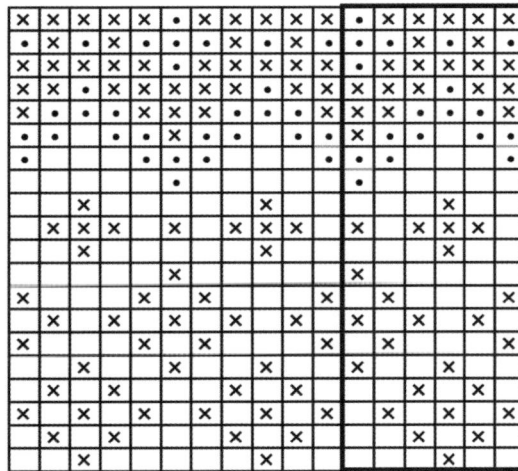

Repeat

Start here for Back, Front and Sleeves

☐ A
☒ B
⊡ C

CHILD'S PATTERNED SWEATER

pattern: model 6 – NB26 (on www.navia.fo)
design: Sigbritt Friis

CHILD'S PATTERNED SWEATER

Difficulty * * *

Sizes 4(6:7:8) years

Chest 64(70:77:83)cm / 25¼(27½:30¼:32¾)in

Length 45(49:53:57)cm / 17¾(19¼:20¾:22½)in

Yarn Navia Uno (50g/1¾oz); in Mid Grey (13), White (11) and Pastel Pink (132)

Quantity
A – Mid Grey, 2(2:3:3) balls
B – White, 1 ball for each size
C – Pastel Pink, 2(2:3:3) balls

Suggested needles 3mm and 3.5mm (UK 11 and 10–9, US 2–3 and 4) circular needles, 60cm (24in) long
3mm and 3.5mm (UK 11 and 10–9, US 2–3 and 4) DPN

Tension (gauge) 25 sts over pattern using 3.5mm (UK 10–9, US 4) needles = 10cm (4in)

Washing Wash the garment in a suitable wool detergent. After washing, spread it out on a towel to dry.

Back and Front　Using 3mm (UK 11, US 2–3) circular needle and yarn A, cast on 140(156:172:188) sts and join to work in the round. Work in k2, p2 rib for 15 rounds.
Change to 3.5mm (UK 10–9, US 4) circular needle and k 1 round, inc evenly by 20 sts over the round (160(176:192:208) sts).
Cont in st st, working pattern from the chart, until work measures 26(30:33:36)cm / 10¼(11¾:13:14¼)in. Maintaining pattern, divide for Back and Front as foll: cast off (bind off) 3 sts, k75(83:91:99) sts, cast off (bind off) 5 sts, k75(83:91:99) sts, cast off (bind off) 2 sts. Cut yarn and leave the work on the needle.

Sleeves (make 2)　Using 3mm (UK 11, US 2–3) DPN and yarn A, cast on 40(40:40:44) sts and join to work in the round. Work in k2, p2 rib for 15 rounds.
Change to 3.5mm (UK 10–9, US 4) DPN and k 1 round, inc evenly by 5(9:13:13) sts over the round (45(49:53:57) sts).
Cont in st st, working pattern from chart, and at same time inc by 1 st and both beg and end of every fifth round until you have 67(73:79:85) sts.
Cont in st st, foll chart, until work measures 33(36:39:42)cm / 13(14¼:15¼:16½)in.
Shape underarms as foll: cast off (bind off) 3 sts, k61(67:73:79), cast off (bind off) 3 sts (61(67:73:79) sts).
Note the pattern on the sleeve must end at same point as pattern on Back and Front.
Place sts on a stitch holder.

Raglan shaping　Arrange the sts of Back, Front and Sleeves on the 3.5mm (UK 10–9, US 4) circular needle as foll: 75(83:91:99) sts for Back, PM, 61(67:73:79) sts for a Sleeve, PM, 75(83:91:99) sts for Front, PM, 61(67:73:79) sts for another Sleeve, PM (272(300:328:356) sts).
Rejoin yarn to beg first round between left sleeve and Front and work 1 round in st st, foll chart.
Maintaining pattern and cont in st st, dec for raglan shaping on every other round as folls:
Next round: (k1, k2tog, k to 3 sts before M, skpo, k1) four times
Next round: k to end.
Rep these 2 rounds until 136(148:160:172) sts rem.
Shape neck as foll: k1, k2tog, k4, cast off (bind off) 13(15:17:19) sts, k to 3 sts before M, skpo, k1, (k1, k2tog, k to 3 sts before M, skpo, k1) three times (115(125:135:145) sts).

Turn and p 1 row (WS).
Maintaining raglan dec on RS rows, cont in st st and working in rows, cast off (bind off) 2(3:3:3) sts at beg of next two rows; cast off (bind off) 2(2:3:3) st at beg of next two rows (91(99:107:117) sts).
P 1 row.
Work one more row of raglan dec (83(91:99:109) sts).
P 1 row.

Neckband Change to 3mm (UK 11, US 2–3) circular needle and using yarn A only, pick up and k 33(33:33:31) sts around neck opening, to end of row and join to work in round (116(124:132:140) sts).
Work in k2, p2 rib for 15 rounds.
Work 15 rounds in k2, p2 rlb, dec evenly by 20(24:28:32) sts over the first round.
Cast off (bind off) loosely in rib.

Finishing Sew together at the underarms.

Chart

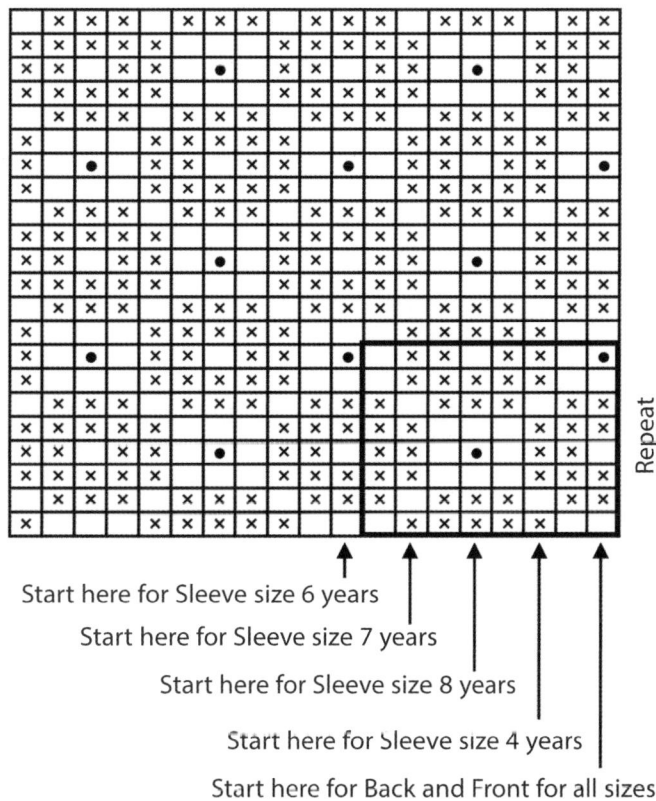

Repeat

Start here for Sleeve size 6 years

Start here for Sleeve size 7 years

Start here for Sleeve size 8 years

Start here for Sleeve size 4 years

Start here for Back and Front for all sizes

☐ A

⊡ B

☒ C

DAISY SWEATER

pattern: model 3 – NB54 (on www.navia.fo)
design: Sára J. Mrdalo

DAISY SWEATER

Difficulty * * * *

Sizes S(M:L:XL)

Bust 102(110:117:125)cm / 40¼(43¼:46:
49¼)in

Length 52(56:60:64)cm / 20½(22:23½:25¼)in

Yarn Navia Trio (50g/1¾oz); in Royal Blue (312)
Navia Alpakka (25g/⅞oz); in Royal Blue (812)
Navia Fípa (50g/1¾oz); in Yellow (1547) and
White (1501)

Quantity
A – Navia Trio, Royal Blue, 5(6:7:8) balls
B – Navia Alpakka, Royal Blue, 3(4:4:5) balls
C – Navia Fípa, Yellow, 1 ball for each size
D – Navia Fípa, White, 1 ball for each size

Suggested needles 5mm and 6mm (UK 6
and 4, US 8 and 10) circular needles, 60cm
(24in) long
6mm (UK 4, US 10) straight needles
5mm and 6mm (UK 6 and 4, US 8 and 10) DPN

Notions Stitch holders
Tapestry needle (darning needle)

Tension (gauge) 13 sts over st st using 6mm
(UK 4, US 10) needles = 10cm (4in)

Note This sweater is knitted using two strands
of yarn – A and B – held together.

Washing Wash the garment in a suitable wool
detergent. After washing, spread it out on a
towel to dry.

Back and Front   Using 5mm (UK 6, US 8) circular
needle and one strand each of yarns A and B, cast
on 132(142:152:162) sts and and join to work in the
round. Work in k1, p1 rib for 9 rounds.
Change to 6mm (UK 4, US 10) circular needle and
work st st until work measures 29(32:35:38)cm /
11½(12½:13¾:15)in.
Divide for Back and Front as foll: cast off 3 sts
k60(65:70:75), cast off (bind off) 6 sts, k60(65:70:75),
cast off (bind off) 3 sts. Turn and cont on first
60(65:70:75) sts for Back; place rem 60(65:70:75) sts
(for Front) on a stitch holder.

Back   Cont in rows in st st and shape armholes
as foll:
P 1 row.
Dec row (RS): k2, k2tog tbl, k to last 6 sts, k2tog, k2.
Rep previous 2 rows until 50(53:58:61) sts rem.**
Cont without shaping until Back measures
23(24:25:26)cm / 9(9½:9¾:10¼)in from armhole.
Place sts on a stitch holder.

Front   Place sts for Front back on needles and rejoin
yarn; work as for Back to **.
Cont without shaping until Front measures
11(12:13:14)cm / 4¼(4¾:5:5½)in from the armhole,
ending on a WS row.
Shape neck as foll: 20(21:23:23), turn and work on
these sts only for left side of neck.
Cast off (bind off) 2 sts at the neck edge on next row.
Cast off (bind off) 1(1:2:2) st(s) at neck edge on foll
alt row. Cast off (bind off) 1 st at neck edge on foll alt
rows until 14(14:15:15) sts rem.
Cont without shaping until left side of Front measures
same as Back.
With RS facing, rejoin yarn and cast off (bind off)
10(11:12:15) sts. Cont in st st for right side of Front,
working dec at neck edge as for left side.
Cont without shaping until right side of Front
measures same as Back.
Transfer the sts for Back to a 6mm (UK 4, US 10)
straight needle, then hold Back and right-hand side
of Front RS tog and work a 3-needle cast off (bind off)
until all the sts of the Front have been cast off. Use the
same technique to join the left-hand side of Front and
Back tog.
Place rem sts for Back on a stitch holder.

Sleeve Using 5mm (UK 6, US 8) circular needle and one strand each of yarns A and B and with RS facing, pick up and k10(12:14:16) sts at top of right armhole, with 5(6:7:8) sts on either side of shoulder seam and beg on Right Back with 4.5(5:5.5:6)cm / 1¾(2:2¼:2¼)in from the seam.

Turn and p 1 row.

Cont to work in rows and in st st, picking up 1 st alt from Back and Right Front at end of each row until there are 52(58:64:70) sts.

Change to 6mm (UK 4, US 10) DPN and join to work in the round.

Cont to work in st st, dec 2 sts at the centre underarm on every sixth(sixth:sixth:fifth) round until 38(40:42:44) sts rem.

Cont in st st until sleeve measures 32(36:40:42)cm / 12½(14¼:15¾:16½)in.

Change to 5mm (UK 6, US 8) DPN and work in k1, p1 rib for 9 rounds.

Cast off (bind off) using an Italian cast-off (bind-off). Rep to add left sleeve.

Neckband Using 5mm (UK 6, US 8) circular needle and one strand each of yarns A and B, pick up and k 58(64:70:74) sts around neckline, including sts rem on stitch holder for Back and join to work in the round.

Work in k1, p1 rib for 9 rounds.

Cast off (bind off) using an Italian cast-off (bind-off).

Embroidery Embroider four daisies, each about 10–11cm (4–4¼in) wide on the Front, just below the neckband. Use Lazy Daisy stitches for the petals, French knots for the centres of the daisies.

Use three strands of C for the petals and three strands of D for the centres of the daisies; work the embroidery using a tapestry needle.

Position the petals in a ring, leaving a space about 4cm (1½in) in the centre.

Lazy Daisy stitch Bring the needle to the front where you want the base of the first petal and pull the yarn through, leaving a long end at the back (to weave in at the end). Insert the needle back in the fabric beside the emerging thread and bring it out to the front of again about 3cm (1½in) away, looping the yarn under the point of the needle. Pull the thread so that the loop lies flat and make a short straight stitch over the loop to hold it in place. Bring the needle out to the front again where you want the second petal to start and make another Lazy Daisy stitch. Continue to work 12 to 16 petals. Weave in the yarn ends to finish.

French knots Bring the needle to the front and pull the yarn through, leaving a long end at the back (to weave in later). Holding the yarn taut with your thumb, wrap it two or three times round the needle. Pull the knot tight around the needle and hold it in place while you twist the needle round and insert it back through the knitting close to where the yarn emerged; pull the yarn through to the wrong side to form the first French knot. Bring the needle out to the front again where you want the next knot to be. Continue to make knots in the same way to fill the centres of the daisies.

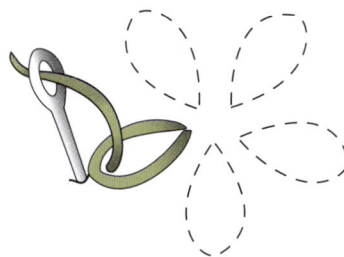

Lazy Daisy stitch

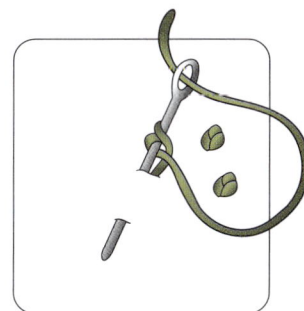

French knots

GEOMETRIC SWEATER

pattern: model 4 – NB54 (on www.navia.fo)
design: Elisabeth Helgadóttir í Gong

GEOMETRIC SWEATER

Difficulty * * * * *

Sizes S(M:L) – the model on pages 142–143 wears a Medium)

Chest/bust 96(102:108)cm / 37¾(40¼:42½)in

Length 56(59:62)cm / 22(23¼:24½)in

Yarn Navia Duo (50g/1¾oz); in White (21) and Olive (253)
Navia Alpakka (25g/⅞oz); in White (801) and in Aqua (848)

Quantity
A – Navia Duo, White, 4(4:5) balls
B – Navia Duo, Olive, 3(3:4) balls
C – Navia Alpakka, White, 4(4:5) balls
D – Navia Alpakka, Aqua, 3(3:4) balls

Suggested needles 4.5mm and 5mm (UK 7 and 6, US 7 and 8) circular needles, 40cm and 60cm (16in and 24in) long
5mm (UK 6, US 8) straight needles
4.5mm and 5mm (UK 7 and 6, US 7 and 8) DPN

Notions Stitch holders

Tension (gauge) 12.5 sts over brioche st pattern using 5mm (UK 6, US 8) needles = 10cm (4in)

Note This sweater uses brioche stitch and is worked by holding two strands of yarn at once; read through the instructions carefully.

Washing Wash the garment in a suitable wool detergent. After washing, spread it out on a towel to dry.

Yarn combinations
AC – one strand yarn A and one strand yarn C
BD – one strand yarn B and one strand yarn D

Brioche stitches
Brioche knit (brk) – k st that was sl in previous row tog with its yo.
Brioche purl (brp) – p st that was sl in previous row tog with its yo.

Brioche stitch worked in rounds
Round 1: using yarn BD, *yo, sl1 purl-wise, p1, rep from * to end of round.
Round 2: using yarn AC, *brk, yo, sl1 purl-wise, rep from * to end of round.
Round 3: using yarn BD, *yo, sl1 purl-wise, brp, rep from * to end of round.
Rep rounds 2 and 3.

Brioche stitch worked in rows
Note you work 2 WS rows, 1 with yarn BD and 1 with yarn AC; then you work 2 right-side rows, 1 one with yarn BD and 1 with yarn AC.
WS:
Row 1: using yarn BD, k1, *yo, sl1 purl-wise, brk, rep from * to last 2 sts, yo, sl1 purl-wise, k1.
Row 2: using yarn AC, k1, *brp, sl1 purl-wise, yo, rep from * to last 2 sts, sl1 purl-wise, k1.
RS:
Row 1: using yarn BD, k1, *ytf, sl1 purl-wise, yo, brp, rep from * to last 2 sts, sl1 purl-wise, yo, k1.
Row 2: using yarn AC, k1, *brk, yo, sl1 purl-wise, rep from * to last 2 sts, brk, k1.

Increase (inc)
K1, but leave the st on needle, yo, k in same st and sl it off needle – you have inc by 2 sts.

Right-leaning decrease (R-dec)
Sl brioche st, brk (the yo and the slipped st tog, lift the sl brioche st over k st, return the sts to left needle, lift the next brioche st over, return the st to right needle and cont – you have now worked 3 sts tog, leaning right.

Left-leaning decrease (L-dec)
Sl the brioche st k-wise, k2tog (the yo, the slipped st and 1 brioche st), lift the sl brioche st over the k st, and cont – you have now worked 3 sts tog, leaning left.

Back and Front   Using 4.5mm (UK 7, US 7) circular needle and yarn AC, use an Italian cast-on (i.e. cast on with a twisted loop rather than a slipknot] to cast on 120(128:136) sts and join to work in the round. Work in k1, p1 rib for 6cm (2¼in).

Change to 5mm (UK 6, US 8) circular needle and work 1 round in k1, p1 rib.

Work in brioche stitch in rounds – see opposite – until work measures 35(36:37)cm / 13¾(14¼:14½)in, finishing with a round 3 (yarn BD).

Divide for Back and Front as foll: cast off (bind off) 3 sts, work 55(59:63) sts, cast off 5 sts, work 55(59:63) sts, cast off (bind off) 2 sts.

Turn and cont on first 53(59:65) sts for Back; place rem 53(59:65) sts (for Front) on a stitch holder.

Back   Cont, working in brioche st in rows – see opposite – until Back measures 9(10:11)cm / 3½(4:4¼)in from the point where Back and Front are divided.

Then work dec and inc on RS with yarn AC as foll: work 15(17:19) sts, R-dec, work 7 sts, inc, work 3 sts, inc, work 7 sts, L-dec, work to end of row.

Work dec and inc in this way on every fourth row six(seven:eight) times, always working 2 sts less before R-dec. (This means you will see more sts in the middle, and fewer at the sides – see photo of Back of sweater.)

Then work dec ONLY as foll: work 4(5:6) sts, L-dec, work 39(43:47) sts, R-dec, work 4(5:6) sts. Work dec in this way on every fourth row a total of seven(eight:nine) times.

Work 1 row in k1, p1 rib in yarn BD.

Cast off (bind off).

Front   Place sts for Front back on needles. Cont, working in brioche st in rows – see above – until Front measures 18(19:20)cm / 7(7½:7¾)in from the point where Back and Front divided, finishing on a RS.

Shape right neck as foll: work 23(25:27) sts in WS Row 1, then work WS Row 2, turn and work RS Row 1.

Dec row (RS): using yarn = AC, k3, L-dec, work to end. Work Dec row every fourth row three(four:five) times. Cont without shaping until Right Front measures 26(28:30)cm / 10¼(11:11¾)in from the point where Back and Front divided. Leave sts on a stitch holder.

With WS facing, rejoin yarn and cast off 7(9:11) sts. Shape left neck as foll: work WS Rows 1 and 2, turn and work RS Row 1.

Dec row (RS): using yarn AC, work 17(19:21) sts, R-dec, p to end.

Complete left neck as for right.

Transfer the sts for Back to a 5mm (UK 6, US 8) straight needle, then hold Back and left-hand side of Front RS tog and work a 3-needle cast off (bind off) until all the sts of the Front have been cast off (bound off). Use the same technique to join the right-hand side of Front and Back tog.

Leave rem sts for Back on a stitch holder.

Sleeves (make 2)   Using 4.5mm (UK 7, US 7) DPN and yarn AC, use an Italian cast-on to cast on 32(36:40) sts and join to work in the round. Work in k1, p1 rib for 6cm (2¼in).

Change to 5mm (UK 6, US 8) DPN, and work 1 round in k1, p1 rib.

Work in brioche stitch in rounds – see opposite – for 6(8:8)cm / 2¼(3¼:3¼)in ending with a round 3.

Inc round: work 1 inc (see above), work to last 2 sts, work 1 inc (36(40:44) sts).

Rep inc round every foll fourteenth(sixteenth: fourteenth) round four(five:six) times (52(60:68) sts). Work without shaping until Sleeve measures 48(51:52)cm / 19(20:20½)in.

Cast off (bind off).

Neckband   Using 4.5mm (UK 7, US 7) circular needle (40cm/16in long) and yarn AC, pick up and k 74(78:82) sts around neckline, including sts rem on stitch holder for Back and join to work in the round.

Work in k1, p1 rib for 8cm (3¼in).

Cast off (bind off) with an Italian cast-off (bind-off) (i.e. sew together the stitches for a neat finish and stretchy edge).

Finishing   Sew in the sleeves.

SWEATER WITH PATTERNED YOKE

pattern: model 2 – NB25 (on www.navia.fo)

design: Tóra Joensen

SWEATER WITH PATTERNED YOKE

Difficulty * * *

Sizes S(M:L)

Chest/bust 88(96:104)cm / 34¾(37¾:41)in

Length 65(69:73)cm / 25½(27¼:28¾)in

Yarn Navia Tradition (50g/1¾oz); in Dark Brown (906), White (901), Mid Grey (903) and Light Brown (905)

Quantity
A – Dark Brown, 4(4:6) balls
B – White, 8(8:12) balls
C – Mid Grey, 2 balls for each size
D – Light Brown, 2 balls for each size

Suggested needles 4.5mm, 5mm and 5.5mm (UK 7, 6 and 5, US 7, 8 and 9) circular needles, 60cm (24in) long
4.5mm, 5mm and 5.5mm (UK 7, 6 and 5, US 7, 8 and 9) DPN

Notions Safety pins
Stitch holders

Tension (gauge) 15 sts over st st pattern using 5mm (UK 6, US 8) needles = 10cm (4in)

Washing Wash the garment in a suitable wool detergent. After washing, spread it out on a towel to dry.

Back and Front   Using 4.5mm (UK 7, US 7) circular needle and yarn A, cast on 132(144:156) sts and join to work in the round. Work in k1, p1 rib for 14 rounds. Change to 5.5mm (UK 5, US 9) circular needle and work in st st foll the pattern from chart 1.
Change to 5mm (UK 6, US 8) circular needle and cont in B, without shaping until work measures 47(51:54)cm / 18½(20:21¼)in.
Divide for Back and Front as foll: place 5 sts on a safety pin, place 56(62:68) sts on a stitch holder, place next 10 sts on a safety pin, place 56(62:68) sts on a stitch holder, place rem 5 sts on a safety pin.
Cut yarn.

Sleeves (make 2)   Using 4.5mm (UK 7, US 7) DPN and yarn A, cast on 32(34:36) sts, and join to work in the round. Work in k1, p1 rib for 14 rounds.
Change to 5.5mm (UK 5, US 9) DPN and and work in st st foll the pattern from chart 1, inc evenly by 5(7:7) sts over the first round (37(41:43) sts).
Change to 5mm (UK 6, US 8) circular needle and cont in st st in yarn B, inc by 1 st at both beg and end of a round every 4cm (1½in) until you have 59(63:67) sts.
Cont in st st without shaping until Sleeve measures 52(55:56)cm / 20½(21¾:22)in. Place first 5 sts and last 5 sts of round on safety pins.

Yoke   Arrange the sts on the 5.5mm (UK 5, US 9) circular needle so you have the sts for Front, for a Sleeve, for Back and for other Sleeve tog on the needle (210(230:250) sts).
Join to work in the round and rejoin yarn B so as to beg between left Sleeve and Front.
Size S only
K 1 round (210 sts).
Size M only
K 1 round, dec evenly by 2 sts over the round (228 sts).
Size L only
K 1 round, dec evenly by 4 sts over the round (246 sts).
K 2 rounds, dec evenly by 3 sts on each round (240 sts).
All sizes
Now work the pattern and dec from chart 2; there should be 70(76:80) sts on the needle when the chart is completed.

Change to 5mm (UK 6, US 8) DPN and work 1 round st st in yarn A, dec by 8(10:10) sts evenly over the round (62(66:70) sts).

Neckband   Change to 4.5mm (UK 7, US 7) DPN and cont in k1, p1 rib for 15 rounds.
Cast off (bind off) loosely in rib.

Finishing   Place the sts of the right armhole and sleeve on two 5mm (UK 6, US 8) DPN and bring them RS tog, then, using yarn B, work a 3-needle cast off (bind off). Rep on left side. Turn under the Neckband and sew loosely in place.

Chart 1

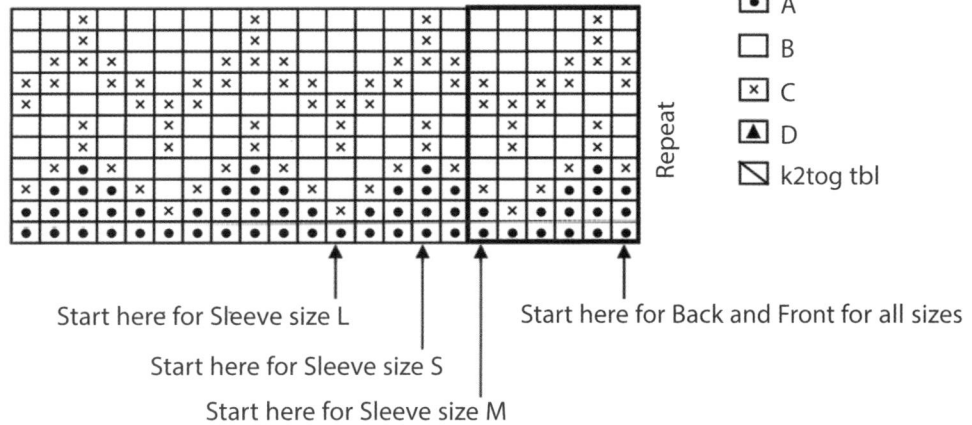

- ⊡ A
- ☐ B
- ⊠ C
- ▲ D
- ◺ k2tog tbl

Repeat

Start here for Sleeve size L
Start here for Sleeve size S
Start here for Sleeve size M
Start here for Back and Front for all sizes

Chart 2

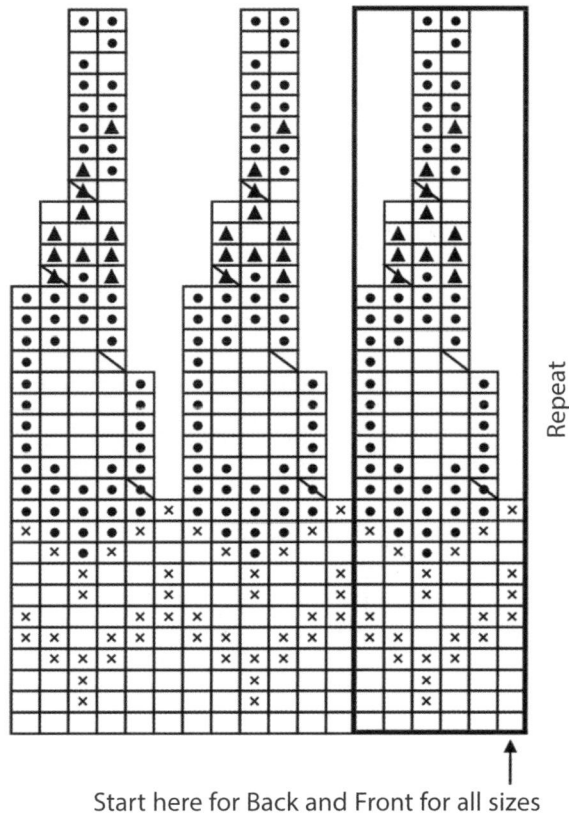

Repeat

Start here for Back and Front for all sizes

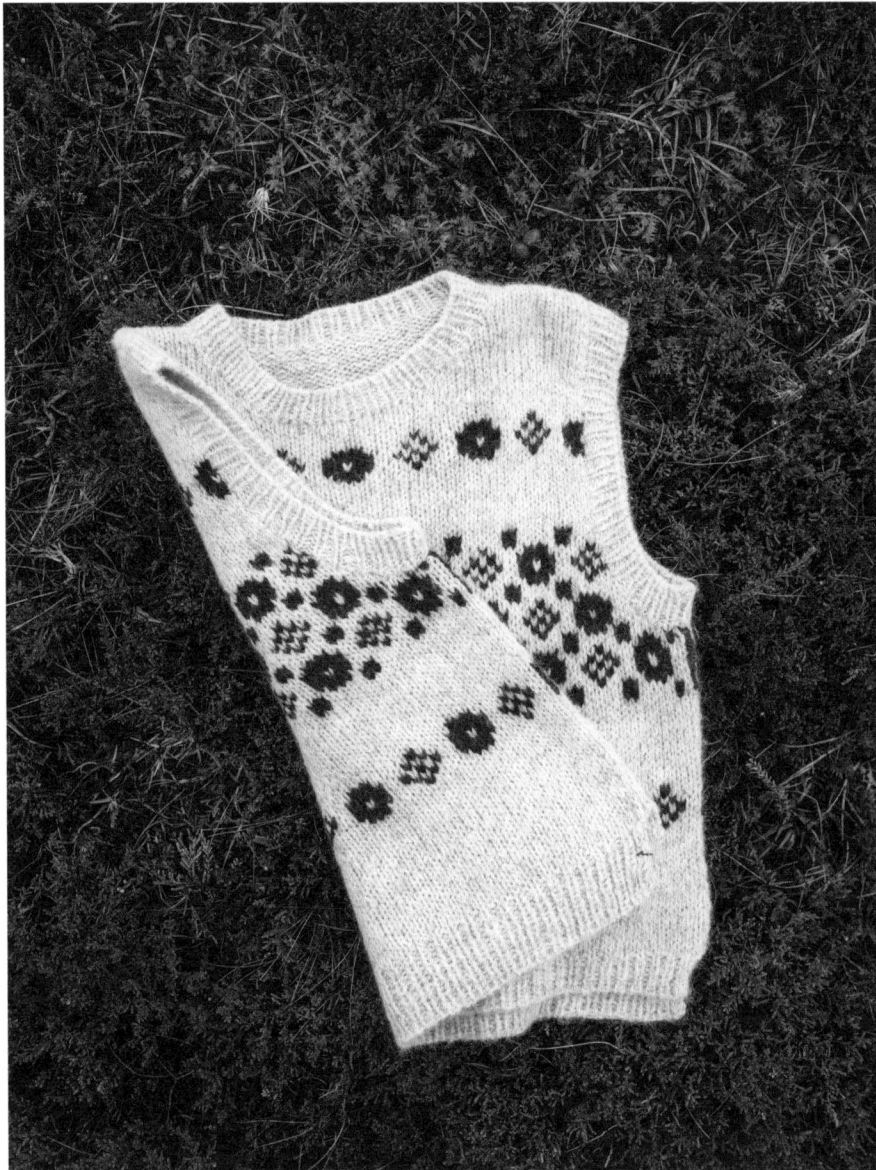

SLEEVELESS SWEATER

pattern: model 1 – NB52 (on www.navia.fo)

design: Sára J. Mrdalo

SLEEVELESS SWEATER

Difficulty * * *

Sizes S(M:L:XL)

Chest/bust 78(89:100:111)cm / 30¾(35:39¼:43¾)in

Front Length 49(52:56.5:60)cm / 19¼(20½:22¼:23½)in

Yarn Navia Duo (50g/1¾oz); in Dark Brown (26) and Sand (28)
Navia Alpakka (25g/⅞oz); in Dark Brown (806) and White (801)

Quantity
A – Navia Duo, Sand, 2(3:3:4) balls
B – Navia Alpakka, White, 2(3:3:4) balls
C – Navia Duo, Dark Brown, 1 for each size
D – Navia Alpakka, Dark Brown, 1 for each size

Suggested needles 3.5mm, 4mm and 4.5mm (UK 10–9, 8 and 7, US 4, 6 and 7) circular needles, 60cm (24in) long
4mm (UK 8, US 6) straight needles
3.5mm (UK 10–9, US 4) DPN

Notions Stitch holders

Tension (gauge) 18 sts over st st pattern using 4mm (UK 8, US 6) needles = 10cm (4in)

Washing Wash the garment in a suitable wool detergent. After washing, spread it out on a towel to dry.

This sweater has slits at the sides, so the ribbing on the Back and Front are worked separately before being joined to work in the round. The ribbing is longer on the Back than on the Front.
You work with two strands of yarn – one of Navia Duo and one of Navia Alpakka.

Back Ribbing Using 3.5mm circular needle (UK 10–9, US 4) and one strand each of yarns A and B, cast on 70(80:90:100) sts and work in k1, p1 rib for 12 rows. Place the sts on a stitch holder.

Front Ribbing Work as for Back Ribbing but work 7 rows in k1, p1 rib.

Back and Front Place the sts of Back and Front ribbing on the 4mm (UK 8, US 6) circular needle and join to work in the round.
Cont in st st until Back measures 11(14:17:19)cm / 4¼(5½:6¾:7½)in. Change to 4.5mm (UK 7, US 7) circular needle and work the pattern from chart 1. Change back to 4mm (UK 8, US 6) needle and work in st st for 5(5.5:6:6)cm / 2(2¼:2½:2½)in more.
Change back to 4.5mm (UK 7, US 7) circular needle and work the pattern from chart 2 until the back measures 25.5(28:32.5:35)cm / 10(11:12¾:13¾)in.
Divide for Back and Front as foll: cast off (bind off) 4 sts, work 61(71:81:91) sts from chart, cast off (bind off) 9 sts, work 61(71:81:91) sts from chart, cast off (bind off) 5 sts.
Turn and cont on first 61(71:81:91) sts for Back; place rem 61(71:81:91) sts (for Front) on a stitch holder.

Back Cont in st st, working in rows and from chart 2, and at the same time, dec by 1 st at each end of every row until 51(59:69:79) rem.
Change to 4mm (UK 8, US 6) circular needle and work in st st for 5(5.5:6:6.5)cm / 2(2¼:2½:2¾)in more.
Change to 4.5mm (UK 7, US 7) needle and work from chart 1.**
Change back to 4mm (UK 8, US 6) needle and work in st st without shaping until Back measures 48(52:56.5:60)cm / 19(20½:22¼:23½)in.
Leave the sts on a stitch holder.

Front Place sts for Front back on needles and rejoin yarn; work as for Back to **.

Change back to 4mm (UK 8, US 6) needle and work in st st without shaping until 40(44:49.5:52.5)cm / 15¾(17¼:19½:20¾)in, ending on a WS row.

Shape neck as foll: k19(22:26:30), turn and work on these sts only for left side of neck.

Cast off (bind off) 1 st at neck edge on every other row until 14(16:19:22) sts rem.

Cont without shaping until left side of Front measures same as Back.

With RS facing, rejoin yarn and cast off (bind off) 13(15:17:19) sts. Cont in st st for right side of neck, working dec at neck edge as for left side.

Cont without shaping until right side of Front measures same as Back.

Transfer the sts for Back to a 4mm (UK 8, US 6) straight needle, then hold Back and right-hand side of Front RS tog and work a 3-needle cast off (bind off) until all the sts of the Front have been cast off (bound off). Use the same technique to join the left-hand side of Front and Back tog.

Leave rem sts for Back on a stitch holder.

Neckband   Using 3.5mm circular needle (UK 10–9, US 4) and one strand each of yarns A and B, pick up and k 74(80:86:92) sts around neckline, including sts rem on stitch holder for Back and join to work in the round.

Work in k1, p1 rib for 7 rounds.

Cast off (bind off) in rib.

Armhole bands   Using 3.5mm circular needle (UK 10–9, US 4) and one strand each of yarns A and B, pick up and k 76(82:88:94) sts around the right armhole edge and join to work in the round.

Work in k1, p1 rib for 7 rounds.

Cast off (bind off) in rib.

Rep to add band to left armhole.

Size S – chart 2

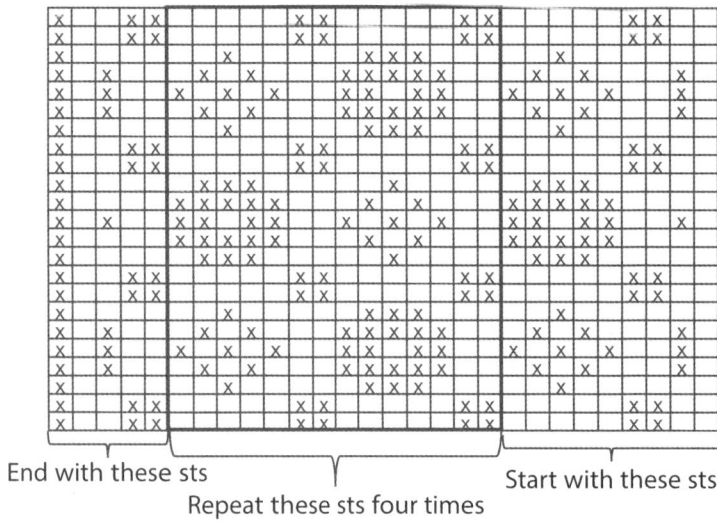

End with these sts

Repeat these sts four times

Start with these sts

Note
The charts on these pages are worked as instructed for the front and then repeated again for the back.

Size S – chart 1

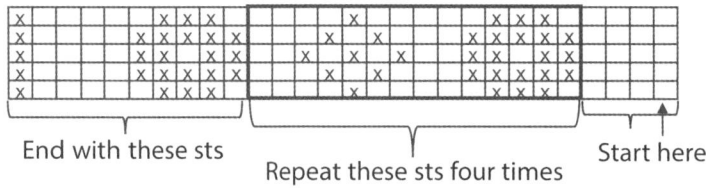

End with these sts

Repeat these sts four times

Start here

Size M – chart 2

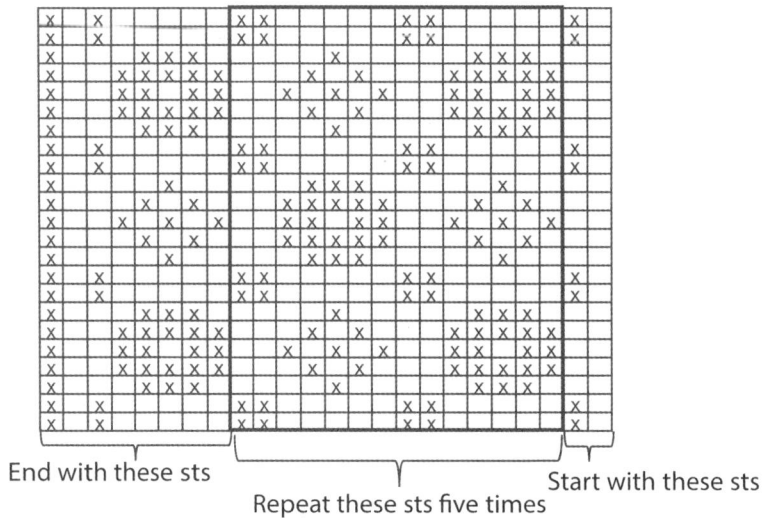

End with these sts

Repeat these sts five times

Start with these sts

Size M – chart 1

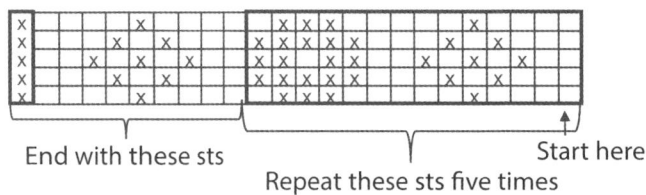

End with these sts

Repeat these sts five times

Start here

Size L – chart 2

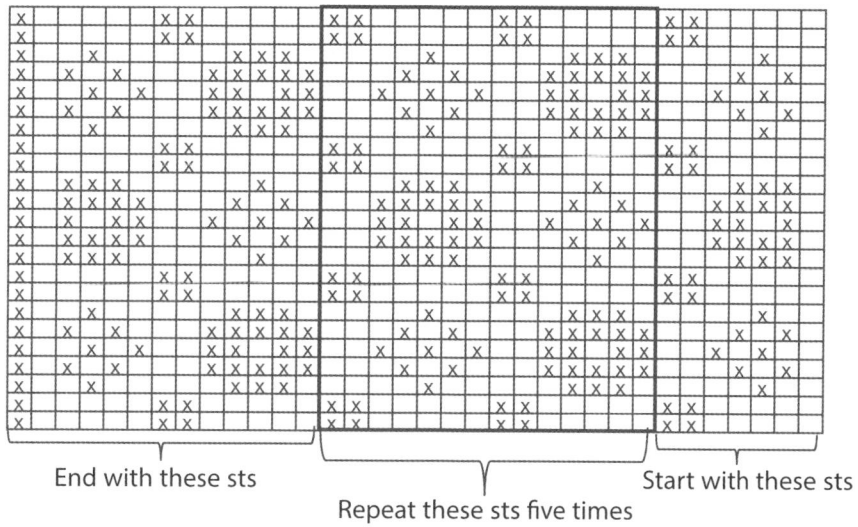

End with these sts

Repeat these sts five times

Start with these sts

Size L – chart 1

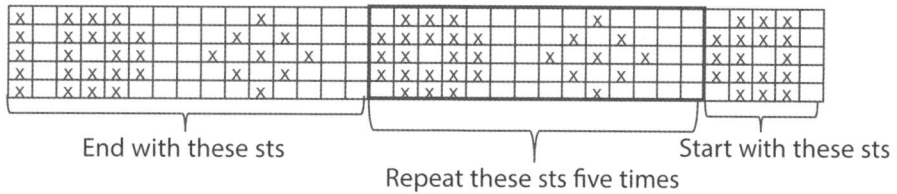

End with these sts

Repeat these sts five times

Start with these sts

Size XL – chart 2

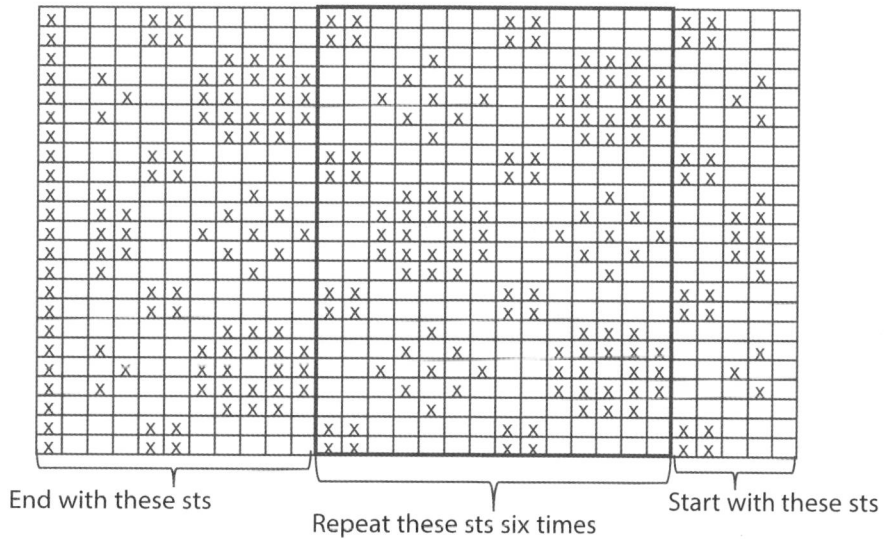

End with these sts

Repeat these sts six times

Start with these sts

Size XL – chart 1

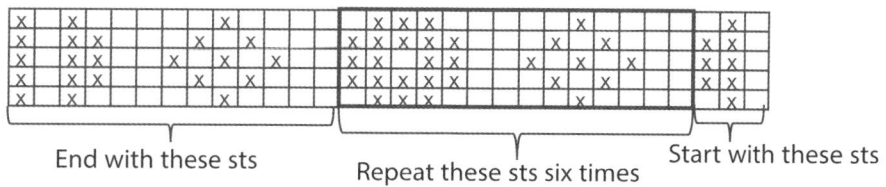

End with these sts

Repeat these sts six times

Start with these sts

159

CARDIGAN WITH PATTERNED YOKE

pattern: model 5 – NB28 (on www.navia.fo)
design: Gunnvør Frederiksberg

CARDIGAN WITH PATTERNED YOKE

Difficulty * * * *

Sizes S(M:L)

Chest/bust 91(96:104)cm / 35¾(38:40¾)in

Length 61(65:69)cm / 24(25½:27¼)in

Yarn Navia Brushed Tradition (50g/1¾oz); in Mid Grey (1103), White (1101) and Dark Brown (1106)

Quantity
A – Mid Grey, 6(6:8) balls
B – White, 2 balls for each size
C – Dark Brown, 2 balls for each size

Suggested needles 4mm (UK 8, US 6) circular needle, 60 or 80cm (24 or 32in) long
4mm (UK 8, US 6) DPN

Notions 10 buttons
Stitch holders
Stitch markers

Tension (gauge) 22 sts over st st pattern using 4mm (UK 8, US 6) needles = 10cm (4in)

Washing Wash the garment in a suitable wool detergent. After washing, spread it out on a towel to dry.

Back and Front   Using 4mm (UK 8, US 6) circular needle and yarn A, cast on 200(212:228) sts and work in k2, p1 rib for 20 rows.
Cont in st st until work measures 37(40:42)cm / 14½(15¾:16½)in, ending on a WS row.
Divide for Back and Fronts as foll: k45(48:53), cast off (bind off) 6 sts, k2tog, k94(100:106), skpo, cast off (bind off) 6 sts, k45(48:53). Leave the sts on the needle.

Sleeves (make 2)   Using 4mm (UK 8, US 6) DPN and yarn A, cast on 45(48:48) sts and join to work in the round. Work in k2, p1 rib for 15 rounds.
Cont in st st, increase by 1 st at both beg and end of every fifth round until there are 72(78:84) sts.
Cont in st st without shaping until work measures 44(47:48)cm / 17¼(18½:19)in. On next round, cast off (bind off) 3 sts at beg and end of round (66(72:78) sts).
Cut yarn and place sts on a stitch holder.

Yoke   Arrange the sts of Back, Front and Sleeves on the 4mm (UK 8, US 6) circular needle as foll: 45(48:53) sts for Left Front, PM, 66(72:78) sts for a Sleeve, PM, 96(102:108) sts for Back, PM, 66(72:78) sts for a Sleeve, PM, 45(48:53) sts for Right Front (318(342:370) sts).
With RS facing, rejoin yarn A to Right Front.
Cont in st st, dec for raglan shaping as foll:
Next row: (k to 2 sts before M, k2tog, skpo) four times (8 sts dec).
Next row: p to end.
Work these 2 rows once(once:three times) (310(334:346) sts).
Commence working from chart, cont in st st and at same time dec for raglan shaping on every RS row until 174(182:186) sts rem.
Shape neck as foll: cont in st st and working from chart, and at same time dec for raglan shaping, cast off (bind off) 3 sts at beg of every row six(six:six) times (132(140:144) sts).
Cast off (bind off).

Neckband   Using 4mm (UK 8, US 6) circular needle and yarn A, with RS facing, pick up and k 150(156:162) sts around neck edge.
P 1 row, dec evenly by 40 sts over the row (110(116:122) sts).
Work in k2, p1 rib for 10 rows.
Cast off (bind off) in rib.

Buttonhole band Using 4mm (UK 8, US 6) circular needle and yarn A, with RS facing, pick up and k 107(116:125) sts along edge of Right Front and work in k2, p1 rib for 4 rows.
Buttonhole row: rib 4, *yo, k2tog, rib 9(10:11) sts, rep from * to last 4 sts, yo, k2tog, rib 2.
Rib 5 more rows
Cast off (bind off) in rib.

Button band Using 4mm (UK 8, US 6) circular needle and yarn A, with RS facing, pick up and k 107(116:125) sts along edge of Left Front and work in k2, p1 rib for 10 rows. Cast off (bind off) in rib.

Finishing Sew the underarm seams. Sew on the buttons to match buttonholes.

Chart

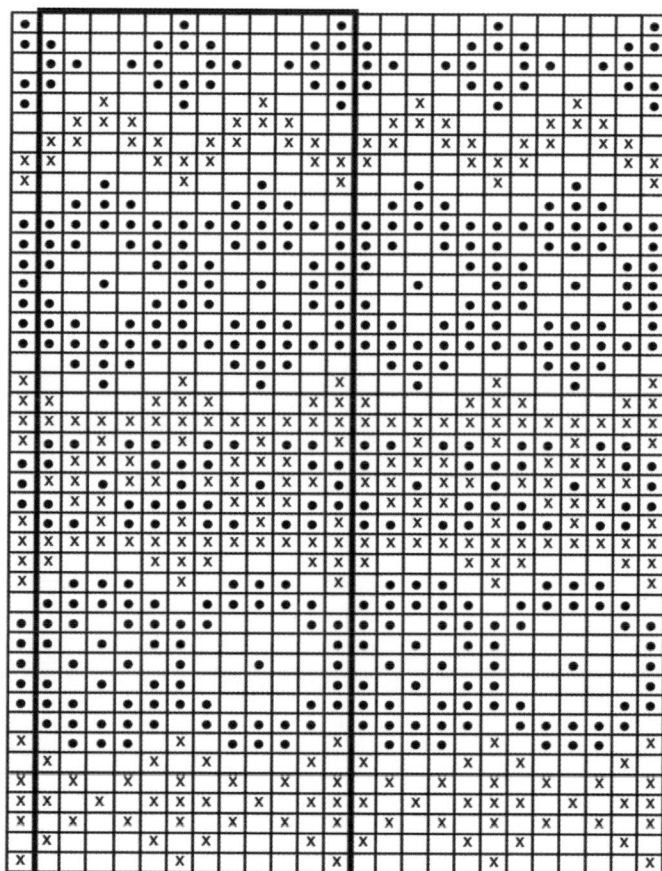

Repeat

☐ A
☒ B
⊡ C

Start here for Back and Sleeves size S

Start here for Left Front size S

Start here for Back and Sleeves size M

Start here for Left Front size M

Start here for Back, Front and Sleeves for size L

LACE-PATTERN SHAWL

pattern: model 5 – NB39 (on www.navia.fo)

LACE-PATTERN SHAWL

Difficulty * * * * *

Width at top about 155cm (61in)

Length at centre about 64cm (25¼in) (not including fringing)

Yarn Navia Uno (50g/1¾oz); in White (11)

Quantity 3 balls

Suggested needles 5.5mm (UK 5, US 9) circular needle, 80cm (32in) long
5.5mm (UK 5, US 9) straight needles
2.5mm (UK 12, US C/2) crochet hook

Notions Stitch markers
Safety pins
Tapestry needle (darning needle)

Tension (gauge) 20 sts over g st pattern using 5.5mm (UK 5, US 9) needles = 10cm (4in)

Washing Wash the garment in a suitable wool detergent. After washing, spread it out on a towel to dry.

Using 5.5mm (UK 5, US 9) circular needle, loosely cast on 359 sts and k 9 rows.
Next row (RS): k4, work first row from chart, k4.
K 1 row.
Cont to foll chart with 4 sts of g st on either side until the chart is completed (269 sts).
K 2 rows.
Next row: k4, k2tog, k112, skpo, PM, k2tog, k27, k2tog, PM, skpo, k to last 6 sts, k2tog, k4 (265 sts).
K 2 rows.
Next row: k4, k2tog, k to M, skpo, sl M, k2tog, k to M, k2tog, sl M, skpo, k to last 6 sts, k2tog, k4 (259 sts).
Rep previous 2 rows until 23 sts rem, remove M.
K 1 row.
Next row: k4, k2tog, k13, skpo, k4 (21 sts).
Next row: k4, then sl these sts on to a safety pin, cast off (bind off) 15 sts, k to end of row.
Next row: k4, turn and work on these 4 sts only.
Work in g st until this strip reaches along length of the 13 cast-off (bound-off) sts.
Place the 4 sts on the safety pin on the other end of the circular needle, then bring the tips of the needles tog so these 4 sts and the 4 sts of the strip are tog, use a tapestry needle (darning needle) to sew the sts together using kitchener stitch (a technique to enable you to invisibly graft together stitches).
Sew the edge of the strip to the cast off (bound off) 13 sts.

Crochet border   Using a 2.5mm (UK 12, US C/2) crochet hook, fasten the yarn at right hand side of top edge of shawl with a sl st. Work *5 ch, 1 tr in first ch, skip 3 rows of knitting, 1 sl st in next row, rep from * to end of top edge, fasten off.

Fringes Cut three strands of yarn 28cm (11in) long. Hold them together and fold in half to form a loop. Use the crochet hook to pull the loop part way through the centre back of the bottom edge of the shawl, then pull the ends of the yarn strands through the loop; pull on the strands to tighten the loop and knot the strands to the shawl. Continue to knot strands along the bottom edge of the shawl, spaced 4 sts apart, in the same way.

*Separate each fringe into groups of three strands and knot these groups together with the adjacent group of three strands. Repeat from * once more. Trim the ends of fringe evenly.

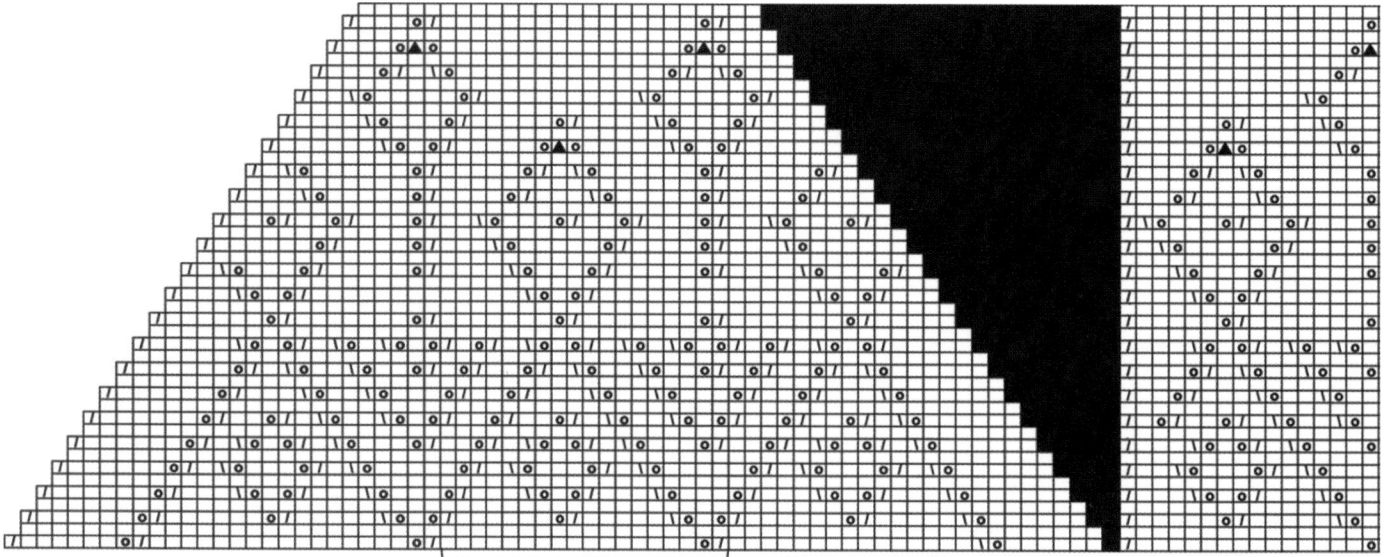

Repeat these sts six times

	yo
	k2tog
	skpo
	sl1, k2tog, psso
	sts that no longer exist after dec

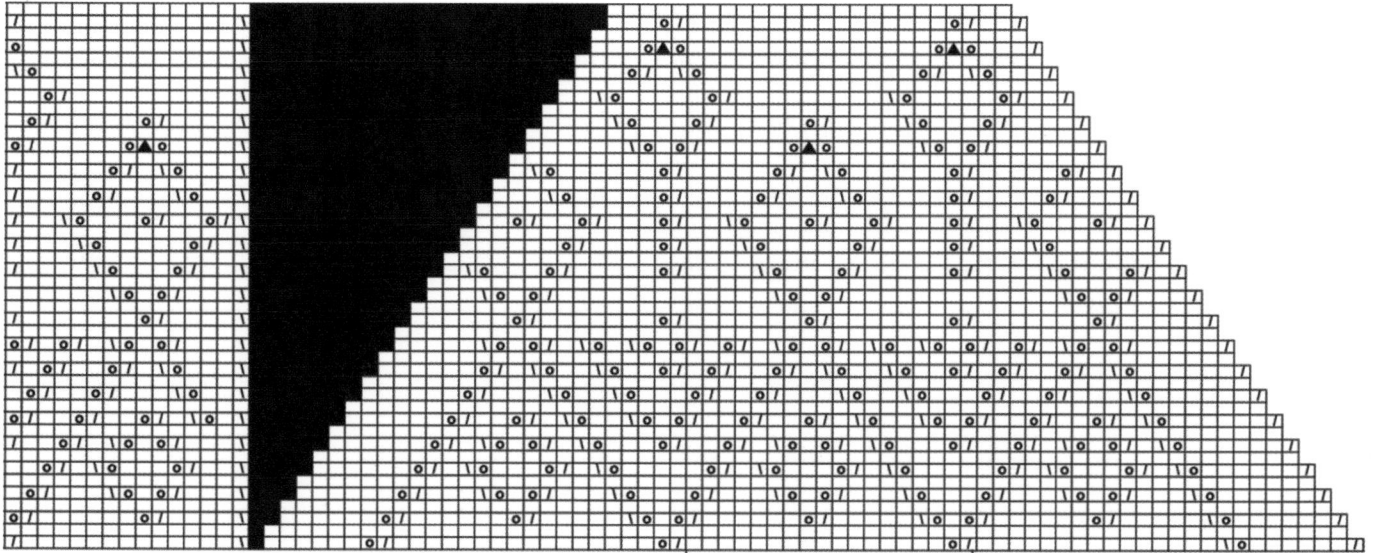

← Cont by working the sts of the next side

Repeat these sts six times

Start here

FESTIVAL SWEATER

pattern: model 11– NB26 (on www.navia.fo)

design: Dagmar Beder

FESTIVAL SWEATER

Difficulty * *

Sizes S(M:L:XL)

Chest/bust 94(102:111:120)cm / 37(40¼:43¾:47¼)in

Length 65(70:72:74)cm / 25½(27½:28¼:29¼)in

Yarn Navia Tradition (50g/1¾oz); in Mid Grey (903), White (901) and Dark Brown (906)

Quantity
A – Mid Grey, 6(6:8:10) balls
B – White, 4 balls for each size
C – Dark Brown, 2(2:4:4) balls

Suggested needles 5mm and 6mm (UK 6 and 4, US 8 and 10) circular needles, 80cm (32in) long
5mm (UK 6, US 8) circular needle, 40cm (16in) long
5mm and 6mm DPN (UK 6 and 4, US 8 and 10)

Notions Stitch holders

Tension (gauge) 14 sts over st st pattern using 4mm (UK 8, US 6) needles = 10cm (4in)

Washing Wash the garment in a suitable wool detergent. After washing, spread it out on a towel to dry.

Back and Front Using 5mm (UK 6, US 8) circular needle, 80cm (32in) long, and yarn B, cast on 132(144:156:168) sts and join to work in the round. Work in k2, p2 rib for 1 round. K 1 round. Cut off yarn B and join on yarn A then cont in k2, p2 rib until work measures 6.5cm (2½in).
Change to 6mm (UK 4, US 10) circular needle and cont in st st, foll chart until work measures 45(49:50:51)cm / 17¾(19¼:19¾:20)in.
While maintaining chart pattern, divide for Back and Front as foll: cast off (bind off) 2 sts, k61(67:73:79), cast off (bind off) 5 sts, k61(67:73:79), cast off (bind off) 3 sts.
Turn and cont on first 61(67:73:79) sts for Back, place rem 61(67:73:79)sts (for Front) on a stitch holder.

Back Cont in st st and foll chart, work in rows without shaping until Back measures 65(70:72:74)cm / 25½(27½:28¼:29¼)in, ending at the point where one of the bands of the design has been completed. Place the sts on a stitch holder.

Front Place sts for Front back on needles and rejoin yarn. Cont in st st and foll chart, work in rows without shaping until Front measures 62(67:69:71)cm / 24½(26½:27¼:28)in, ending on a WS row.
Shape neck as foll: k21(23:25:28), turn and work on these sts only for left side of neck.
At same time as working in st st and foll chart, cast off (bind off) 2 sts at beg of next row, 1(2:3:3) st(s) at beg of foll alt row (18(19:20:23) sts).
Cont in st st, foll chart, without shaping until left side of Front measures the same as Back, ending in same position on chart. Cut yarn and place sts on a stitch holder.
With RS facing, place next 19(21:23:23) sts on a holder for the neck. Rejoin yarn to rem 21(23:25:28)sts and work dec at neck edge as for left side of neck, and at same time work in st st and foll chart.
Cont without shaping until right side of Front measures the same as Back, ending in same position on chart.
Transfer the sts for the Back to a 6mm (UK 5, US 9) straight needle, then hold Back and right-hand side of Front RS tog and work a 3-needle cast off (bind off) until all the sts of the Front have been cast off (bound off). Use the same technique to join the left-hand side of Front and Back tog.

Chart

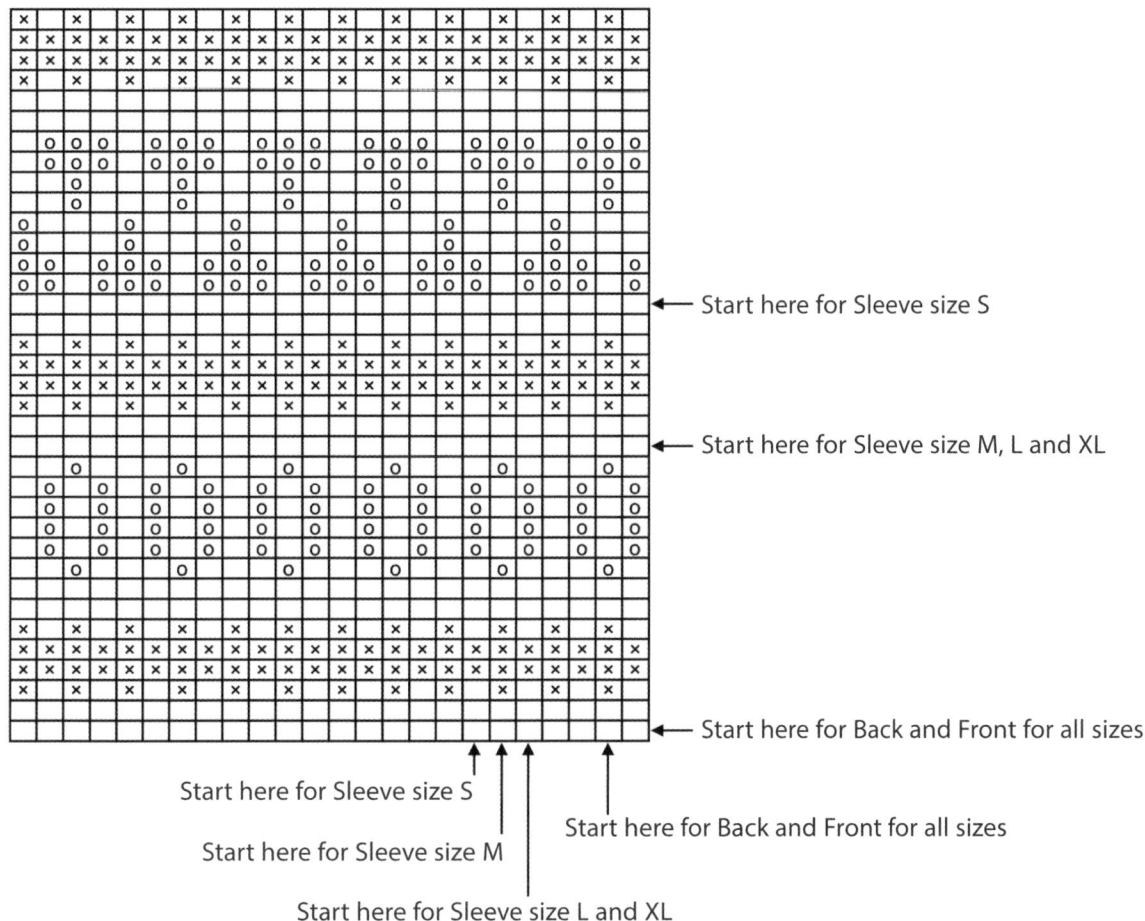

→ Start here for Sleeve size S

→ Start here for Sleeve size M, L and XL

→ Start here for Back and Front for all sizes

Start here for Sleeve size S

Start here for Sleeve size M

Start here for Sleeve size L and XL

Start here for Back and Front for all sizes

☐ A   ◉ B   ☒ C

Sleeves (make 2)   Using 5mm (UK 6, US 8) DPN and yarn B, cast on 28(28:32:32) sts and join to work in the round. Work in k2, p2 rib for 1 round. K 1 round. Cut yarn B and join in yarn A and cont in k2, p2 rib until work measures 6.5cm (2½in).
Change to 6mm (UK 4, US 10) DPN and cont in st st, foll chart, but work the centre underarm st in yarn A all the way up the sleeve. At the same time, inc by 1 st on each side of the centre underarm stitch on fourth round, then on every sixth round until there are 54(58:62:66) sts. Cont in st st, foll chart and without shaping until sleeve measures 51(54:56:57)cm / 20(21¼:22:22½)in and you are three rounds short of

the point where one of the bands of the design would be completed. Cast off (bind off) the centre st at the underarm, then turn and work 3 rows from the chart in st st. Cast off (bind off).

Neckband   Using 5mm (UK 6, US 8) circular needle 40cm (16in) and yarn A, pick up and k 64(68:72:76) sts around the neck and work in k2, p2 rib for 18cm (7in). Change to yarn B and p 1 round, then work 1 round in k2, p2 rib. Cast off (bind off).

Finishing   Sew in the sleeves.

CHILD'S WAVE CARDIGAN

pattern: model 6 – NB55 (on www.navia.fo)

design: Gunnvør Frederiksberg

CHILD'S WAVE CARDIGAN

Difficulty * * * *

Sizes 1(2:4:5–6) years

Chest 52(56:60:64)cm / 20½(22:23½:25¼)in

Length 32(36:41:46)cm / 12½(14¼:16¼:18)in

Yarn Navia Duo (50g/1¾oz); in Royal Blue (212)

Quantity 3(3:4:4) balls

Suggested needles 3.5 and 4mm (UK 10–9 and 8, US 4 and 6) circular needles, 60 or 80cm (24 or 32in) long
3.5 and 4mm (UK 10–9 and 8, US 4 and 6) DPN

Notions 5(6:7:8) buttons
Stitch holders
Stitch markers
Safety pins

Tension (gauge) 30 sts over st st using 3.5mm (UK 10–9, US 4) needles = 10cm (4in)

Washing Wash the garment in a suitable wool detergent. After washing, spread it out on a towel to dry.

Back and Front Using 3.5mm (UK 10–9, US 4) circular needle, cast on 156(168:180:192) sts.
Row 1 (RS): sl1, k5, p1, *k2, p2, rep from * to last 7 sts, p1, k5, p1.
Row 2 (WS): sl1, k6, *k2, p2, rep from * to last 7 sts, k6, p1.
Rep these 2 rows twice more.
Buttonhole row (RS): sl1, k2, yo, k2tog, k1, p1, *k2, p2, rep from * to last 6 sts, p1, k5, p1.
Rep row 2, inc by 2 sts evenly spaced across the row. (158(170:182:194) sts).
Change to 4mm (UK 8, US 6) circular needle.
Next row (RS): sl1, k5, p1, work from chart to last 7 sts, p1, k5, p1.
Next row (WS): sl1, k6, work from chart to last 7 sts, k6, p1.
Rep these two rows until work measures 19(22:26:30)cm / 7½(8¾:10¼:11¾)in and at the same time, work Buttonhole row over first 7 sts on RS every 4cm (1½in). (The last buttonhole will be worked in the ribbing of Neckband.)
Maintaining pattern, divide for Back and Fronts as foll: work 40(43:46:49) sts, cast off (bind off) 6 sts, work 66(72:78:84) sts, cast off (bind off) 6 sts, work 40(43:46:49) sts. Leave the work on the needle.

Sleeves (make 2) Using 3.5mm (UK 10–9, US 4) DPN, cast on 32(32:36:40) sts and join to work in the round. Work k2, p2 rib for 8 rounds, inc by 6(8:8:8) sts evenly spaced across the round (38:40:44:48) sts).
Change to 4mm (UK 8, US 6) DPN and cont in st st, inc by 1 st at both ends of a round every 2cm (¾in) until there are 52(58:64:70) sts.
Cont in st st without shaping until work measures 19(22:25:28)cm / 7½(8¾:9¾:11)in.
Cast off (bind off) 3 sts at both ends of next round (46(52:58:64) sts). Leave sts on a stitch holder.

Raglan shaping Arrange the sts of Back, Fronts and Sleeves on the 4mm (UK 8, US 6) circular needle as foll: 40(43:46:49) sts for Left Front, PM, 46(52:58:64) sts for a Sleeve, PM, 66(72:78:84) sts for Back, PM, 46(52:58:64) sts for a Sleeve, PM, 40(43:46:49) sts for Right Front (238(262:286:310) sts).
With RS facing, rejoin yarn to Right Front and work raglan dec as foll (cont to work evenly spaced Buttonhole rows on RS as before):

Next row (RS): sl1, k5, p1, (work from chart to 3 sts before M, k2tog tbl, p1, sl M, p1, k2tog, k to 3 sts before M, k2tog tbl, p1, sl M, p1, k2 tog) twice, work from chart to last 7 sts, p1, k5, p1.

Next row (WS): sl1, k6, (work from chart to M, sl M, p to M, sl M) twice, work from chart to last 7 sts, k6, p1. Rep these 2 rows until 158(166:174:182) sts rem. Shape neck as foll:

Next row (RS): sl1, k5, then place these 6 sts on a safety pin, cast off (bind off) 2 sts, (work from chart to 3 sts before M, k2tog tbl, p1, sl M, p1, k2tog, k to 3 sts before marker, k2tog tbl, p1, sl M, p1, k2tog) twice, work from chart to last 6 sts, (cast off/bind off the sts at the beg of next row), then place rem 6 sts on a safety pin.

Next row: cast off (bind off) 2 sts, (work from chart to M, sl M, p to M, sl M) twice, work from chart to end of row.

Cont to work from chart for Fronts and Back and in st st on Sleeves, cast off (bind off) 2 sts at beg of every row four(six:eight:ten) times (134(138:142:146) sts). Cut yarn.

Neckband Change to 3.5mm (UK 10–9, US 4) circular needle, and place the sts on safety pins back on either end of the needle.

Rejoin yarn and k over first 6 sts, then pick up and k 5(7:8:9) sts over cast-off (bound-off) sts at neck, k across 134(138:142:146) sts on needle, pick up and k 5(7:8:9) sts over cast-off (bound-off) sts at other side of neck, then k over last 6 sts (156(164:170:176) sts). Work in k2, p2 rib for 9 rows, dec by 56(56:54:56) sts evenly over first row (100(108:116:120) sts) and adding a buttonhole as described above on row 4 or 5.

Cast off (bind off) in rib.

Finishing Sew the underarms together. Sew on the buttons to match the buttonholes.

Chart for the wave pattern

Repeat

C6B – slip 3 sts onto cable needle, hold at back, k3, k3 sts from cable needle

C6F – slip 3 sts onto cable needle, hold at front, k3, k3 sts from cable needle

LEAF-PATTERN SWEATER

pattern: model 2 – NB63 (on www.navia.fo)
design: Sára J. Mrdalo

LEAF-PATTERN SWEATER

Difficulty * * * *

Sizes XS/S(M:L:XL:XXL)

Bust 93(102:115:128:142)cm /
36½(40¼:45¼:50½:56)in

Length 48(52:54:57:59)cm /
19(20½:21¼:22½:23¼)in

Yarn Navia Fípa (50g/1¾oz); in White (1501)

Quantity 4(4:5:6:8) balls

Suggested needles 7mm, 10mm and 15mm
(UK 2, 000 and no equivalent size; US 10½–11,
15 and 19) circular needles, 60cm (24in) long,
7mm (UK 2, US 10½–11) straight needles
7mm (UK 2, US 10½–11) DPN

Notions Stitch holders

Tension (gauge) 9 sts over st st using 10mm
(UK 000, US 15) needles = 10cm (4in)

Washing Wash the garment in a suitable wool
detergent. After washing, spread it out on a
towel to dry.

Back and Front   Using 7mm (UK 2, US 10½–11)
circular needle, cast on 84(92:104:116:128) sts and join
to work in the round. Work in k2, p2 rib for 10 rounds.
Change to 10mm (UK 000, US 15) circular needle and
set the position of the pattern as foll: k5(7:10:13:16),
p1, work 30 sts from chart, p1, k47(53:62:71:80).
Cont in this way until work measures
27(30:31:33:34)cm / 10¾(11¾:12¼:13:13½)in.
Maintaining pattern, divide for Back and Front as foll:
cast off (bind off) 1 st, work 39(43:49:55:61) sts, cast
off (bind off) 3 sts, work 39(43:49:55:61) sts, cast off
(bind off) 2 sts.
Place the 39(43:49:55:61) sts for Front (with
leaf pattern) on a stitch holder. Cont on rem
39(43:49:55:61) sts (in st st) for Back.

Back   Cont in rows and at same time, cast
off (bind off) 1 st at beg of every row until
29(33:39:45:51) sts rem.**
Cont without shaping until Back measures
48(52:54:57:59)cm / 19(20½:21¼:22½:23¼)in. Place
the sts on a stitch holder.

Front   Place sts for Front back on needles and rejoin
yarn. Maintaining pattern, work as for Back to **.
Cont without shaping until Front measures
43(46:47:49:51)cm / 17(18:18½:19¼:20)in ending on a
WS row.
Shape neck as foll: work 10(11:13:16:18) sts, turn and
work on these sts only for left side of neck.
Maintaining pattern, cast off (bind off) 1 st at the neck
edge on every other row two(three:three:four:four)
times (8(8:10:12:14) sts).
Cont without shaping until left side of Front measures
same as Back; cut yarn.
With RS facing, rejoin yarn and cast off (bind off)
9(11:13:13:15) sts. Maintaining pattern, cont for right
side of Front, working dec at neck edge as for left
side. Cont without shaping until right side of Front
measures same as Back.
Transfer the sts for Back to a 7mm (UK 2, US 10½–11)
straight needle, then hold Back and right-hand side
of Front RS tog and work a 3-needle cast off (bind off)
until all the sts of the Front have been cast off. Use the
same technique to join the left-hand side of Front and
Back tog.
Place rem sts for Back on a stitch holder.

Sleeve Using 15mm (UK – no equivalent, US 19) circular needle, pick up and k 10(14:18:22:26) sts at top of right armhole, beg 5(7:9:11:13) sts on either side of shoulder seam and about 4.5(5:5.5:6:6.5)cm / 1¾(2:2¼:2½:2¾)in from the seam.
Turn and p 1 row.
Cont to work in rows and in st st, picking up 1 st alt from Back and Right Front at end of each row until there are 26(32:38:42:46) sts and the sleeve fits the armhole.
Join to work in the round and cont in st st until sleeve measures 35(38:37:35:34)cm / 13¾(15:14½:13¾:13½)in from armhole.
Sizes L, XL and XXL only
At the same time, dec by 1 st at each end of every fourth(fourth:third) until 32 sts rem.
All sizes
K 1 round, dec by 6(8:8:8:8) sts evenly spaced over the round.

Change to 7mm (UK 2, US10½–11) DPN and work in k2, p2 rib for 10 rounds.
Cast off (bind off) in rib.
Add left sleeve in the same way.

Neckband Using 7mm (UK 2, US 10½–11) DPN, pick up and k 44(48:54:60:66) sts around neckline, including sts rem on stitch holder for Back.
Join to work in the round and work in k2, p2 rib for 1 round.
Sizes L, XL and XXL only
Dec by 2(4:10) sts on this round, evenly spaced over the round (52(56:56) sts).
All sizes
Work in rib for 9 more rounds.
Cast off in rib.

Chart for the leaf pattern

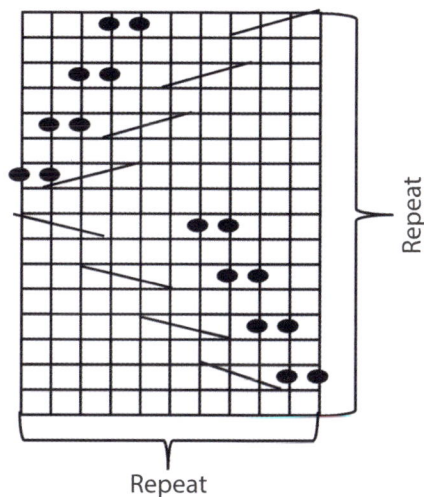

Repeat

Repeat

☐ k on RS, p on WS

sl2, k1, psso

k3tog

● yo between sts

CHILD'S LEAF-PATTERN SWEATER

pattern: model 3 – NB66 (on www.navia.fo)

design: Sára J. Mrdalo

CHILD'S LEAF-PATTERN SWEATER

Difficulty * * * *

Sizes 6(8:9:10) years

Chest 76(82:88:92)cm / 30(32¼:34¾:36¼)in

Length 37(41:45:50)cm / 14½(16¼:17¾:19¾)in

Yarn Navia Fípa (50g/1¾oz); in Amazonite (1530)

Quantity 3(4:4:5) balls

Suggested needles 5.5mm, 9mm and 12mm circular needles (UK 5, 00,(no equivalent size); US 9, 13 and 17), 60cm (24in) long 9mm (UK 00, US 13) straight needles

Notions Stitch holders

Tension (gauge) 8 sts over rev st st using 9mm (UK 00, US 13) needles = 10cm (4in)

Special abbreviation rev st st = reverse stocking (stockinette) stitch (p on RS, k on WS)

Washing Wash the garment in a suitable wool detergent. After washing, spread it out on a towel to dry.

Back and Front   Using 5.5mm (UK 5, US 9) circular needle, cast on 80(88:96:104) sts and join to work in the round. Work in k2, p2 rib for 10 rounds.
Change to 9mm (UK 00, US 13) circular needle and set the position of the pattern as foll: p10(12:14:11), work 20(20:20:30) sts from chart, p20(24:28:22), work 20(20:20:30) sts from chart, p10(12:14:11).
Cont in this way until work measures 24(28:31:35)cm / 9½(11:12¼:13¾)in.
Maintaining pattern, divide for Back and Front as foll: cast off (bind off) 3 sts, work 34(38:42:46) sts, cast off (bind off) 6 sts, work 34(38:42:46) sts, cast off (bind off) 3 sts.
Turn and cont on first 34(38:42:46) sts for Back, place rem 34(38:42:46) sts (for Front) on a stitch holder.

Back   Cont in rows, maintaining pattern and panels of rev st st on either side, and at same time, cast off (bind off) 1 st at beg of every row until 28(32:34:38) sts rem.**
Cont without shaping until Back measures 12(13:14:15)cm / 4¾(5:5½:6)in from the point where Back and Front were divided. Place the sts on a stitch holder.

Front   Place sts for Front back on needles and rejoin yarn. Maintaining pattern, work as for Back to **.
Cont without shaping until Front measures 7(7.5:8:9)cm / 2¾(3:3¼:3½)in from the point where Back and Front were divided.
Shape neck as foll: work 10(12:12:14) sts, turn and work on these sts only for left side of neck.
Maintaining pattern, cast off (bind off) 1 st at the neck edge on every other row three times (7(9:9:11) sts).
Cont without shaping until left side of Front measures same as Back; cut yarn.
With RS facing, rejoin yarn and cast off (bind off) 8(8:10:10) sts. Maintaining pattern, cont for right side of Front, working dec at neck edge as for left side. Cont without shaping until right side of Front measures same as Back.
Transfer the sts for Back to a 9mm (UK 00, US 13) straight needle, then hold Back and right-hand side of Front RS tog and work a 3-needle cast off (bind off) until all the sts of the Front have been cast off. Use the same technique to join the left-hand side of Front and Back tog.
Place rem sts for Back on a stitch holder.

Sleeve   Using 12mm (UK – no equivalent, US 17) circular needle, pick up and k 8 sts at top of right armhole, about 3cm (1¼in) from the shoulder seam. Turn and k 1 row.
Cont to work in rows and in g st, picking up 1 st alt from Back and Right Front at end of each row until there are 32(40:48:56) sts and the sleeve fits the armhole.
Work in rows in g st, dec by 1 st at each end of every tenth(ninth:sixth:fifth) row until 26(32:38:44) sts rem.
Cont in g st until work measures 21(26:30:34)cm / 8¼(10¼:11¾:13½)in.
K 1 row, dec evenly by 6(12:14:20) sts across the row (20(20:24:24) sts).
Change to 5.5mm (UK 5, US 9) needle and in k2, p2 rib for 10 rounds.
Cast off (bind off) in rib.
Add left sleeve in the same way.

Neckband   Using 5.5mm (UK 5, US 9) circular needle, pick up and k 44(48:52:56) sts around the neck edge, including sts rem on stitch holder for Back.
Join to work in the round and work in k2, p2 rib for 10 rounds.
Cast off (bind off) in rib.

Finishing   Sew the sleeve seams.

Chart for the leaf pattern

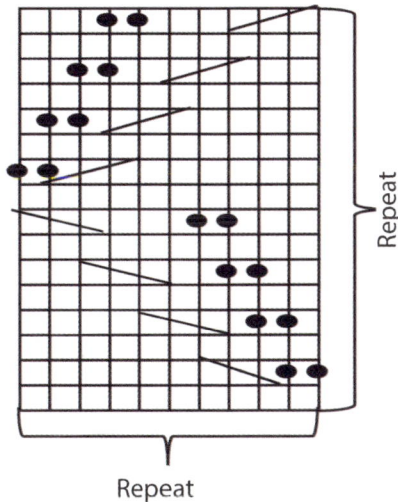

Repeat

Repeat

☐ k on RS, p on WS

▱ sl2, k1, psso

▱ k3tog

● yo between sts

BABY SWEATER AND LEGGINGS

pattern: model 1 – NB37 (on www.navia.fo)
design: Sára J. Mrdalo

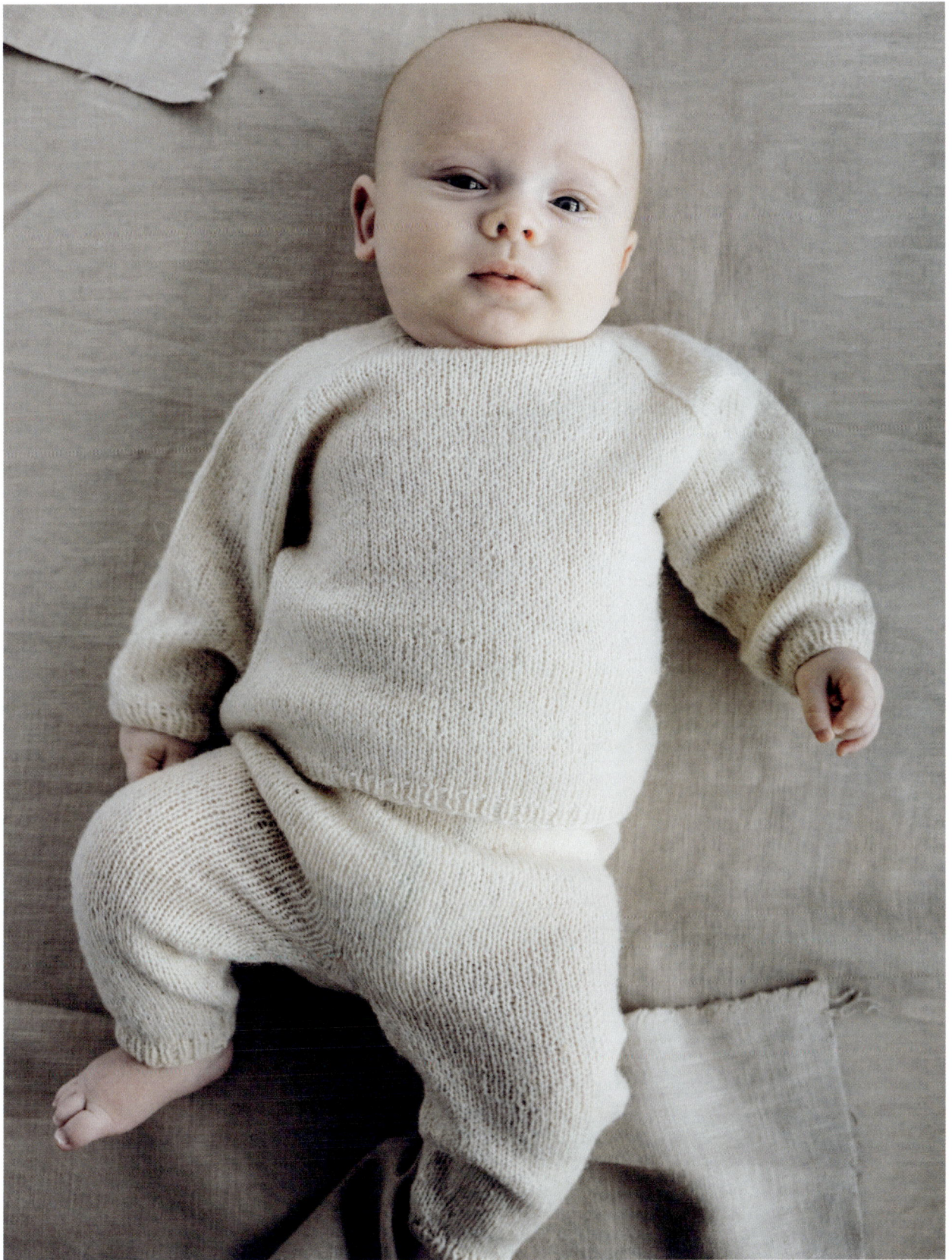

SWEATER

Difficulty * * *

Sizes 3(3–6:9–12) months

Chest 52(57:62)cm / 20½(22½:24½)in

Length 27(32:37)cm / 10¾(12½:14½)in

Yarn Navia Uno (50g/1¾oz); in White (11)

Quantity 2(2:3) balls

Suggested needles 3.5mm and 4mm (UK 10–9 and 8, US 4 and 6) circular needles, 40cm (16in) long
4mm (UK 8, US 6) circular needle, 60cm (24in) long
3.5mm and 4mm (UK 10–9 and 8, US 4 and 6) DPN

Notions Stitch holders

Tension (gauge) 25 sts over st st using 4mm (UK 8, US 6) needles = 10cm (4in)

Washing Wash the garment in a suitable wool detergent. After washing, spread it out on a towel to dry.

Back and Front   Using 3.5mm (UK 10–9, US 4) circular needle, cast on 130(142:154) sts and join to work in the round. Work in k1, p1 rib for 5 rounds. Change to 4mm (UK 8, US 6) circular needle, 60cm (24in) long, and cont in st st until work measures 14(18:22)cm / 5½(7:8¾)in.
Divide for Back and Front as foll: k61(65:71) sts, cast off (bind off) 4(6:6) sts, k61(65:71) sts, cast off (bind off) 4(6:6) sts. Leave the work on the needle.

Sleeves (make 2)   Using 3.5mm (UK 10–9, US 4) DPN cast on 40(44:46) sts and join to work in the round. Work in k1, p1 rib for 5 rounds.
Change to 4mm (UK 8, US 6) DPN and cont in st st, inc by 1 st at each end of every sixth round until you have 54(60:64) sts.
Cont in st st until sleeve measures 13(15:17)cm / 5(6:6¾)in.
Cast off (bind off) 2(3:3) sts at beg and end of next round. Place rem 50(54:58) sts on a stitch holder.

Raglan shaping   Arrange the sts of Back, Front and Sleeves on the 4mm (UK 8, US 6) circular needle as foll: 61(65:71) sts for Back, 50(54:58) sts for Sleeve, 61(65:71) sts for Front, 50(54:58) sts for Sleeve (222(238:258) sts). Rejoin yarn to beg first round between left Sleeve and Front.
Next round: (k2tog, k59(63:69), PM, k2tog, k48(52:56), PM) twice (218(234:254) sts).
K 2 rounds.
Dec for raglan shaping as foll:
Next round: (k to 2 sts before M, sl2 sts k-wise, remove M, k1, psso, replace M) four times.
Next round: k to end.
Rep these 2 rounds until 90(90:94) sts rem.
Shape neck as foll: k8(8:7), place next 12(12:16) sts on a stitch holder, cont to end of round, working raglan dec as before (70 sts).
P 1 row.
Cont in rows, maintaining raglan dec on RS rows and at same time cast off (bind off) 1 st at beg of row six times (40 sts).

Neckband   Change to 3.5mm (UK 10–9, US 4) DPN and pick up and k 32(34:38) sts round neck (72(74:78) sts). Join to work in the round and work in k1, p1 rib for 5 rounds. Cast off (bind off) loosely in rib.

Finishing   Sew the underarms together.

LEGGINGS

Difficulty * * *

Sizes 3(3–6:9–12) months

Hips: 44(50:54)cm / 17¼(19¾:21¼)in

Leg Length 18(22:25)cm / 7(8¾:9¾)in

Yarn Navia Uno (50g/1¾oz); in White (11)

Quantity 1(2:2) balls

Suggested needles 3.5mm and 4mm
(UK 10–9 and 8, US 4 and 6) circular needles,
40cm (16in) long
3.5mm (UK 10–9, US 4) DPN

Notions 50cm (20in) elastic
Stitch holders

Tension (gauge) 25 sts over st st using 4mm
(UK 8, US 6) needles = 10cm (4in)

Washing Wash the garment in a suitable wool
detergent. After washing, spread it out on a
towel to dry.

Body Using 3.5mm (UK 10–9, US 4) circular needle,
cast on 112(124:136) sts and join to work in the round.
Work in k1, p1 rib for 12 rounds, p 1 round, then work
12 more rounds in k1, p1 rib.
Change to 4mm (UK 8, US 6) circular needle and
k 1 round. PM at beg of next round and shape
centre-back as foll, keeping M in position as you
work: k7(8:9), turn, p15(16:17), turn, k23(24:25), turn,
p31(32:33), turn, k39(40:41), turn, p47(48:49), turn
and cont working in round until the work measures
23(24:26)cm / 9(9½:10¼)in at the centre back.

Gusset K56(62:68), PM, k to M at centre back.
Cont to work in round in st st, inc by 1 st on either
side of each M on every third round until there are
124(136:152) sts. K 1 round, dec by 2 sts on either side
of each M.
Divide work at centre-front and -back, placing one set
of sts on a stitch holder; 58(64:72) sts rem on needle.

Legs Divide the sts bet 4mm (UK 8, US 6) DPN and
join to work in the round. Cont in st st, dec by 2 sts at
inside of leg on every fifth round until 32(32:40) sts
rem. Cont in st st without shaping until leg measures
18(20:22)cm / 7(7¾:8¾)in. Change to 3.5mm (UK 10–9,
US 4) DPN and work in k1, p1 rib for 5 rounds. Cast off
(bind off) in rib.
Divide sts on stitch holder bet 4mm (UK 8, US 6) DPN
and work second leg to match first.

Finishing Sew the gusset together. Fold under
top edge and sew in place, leaving an opening for
inserting the elastic. Thread the elastic through the
turning, adjust the length and secure, then sew the
opening closed.

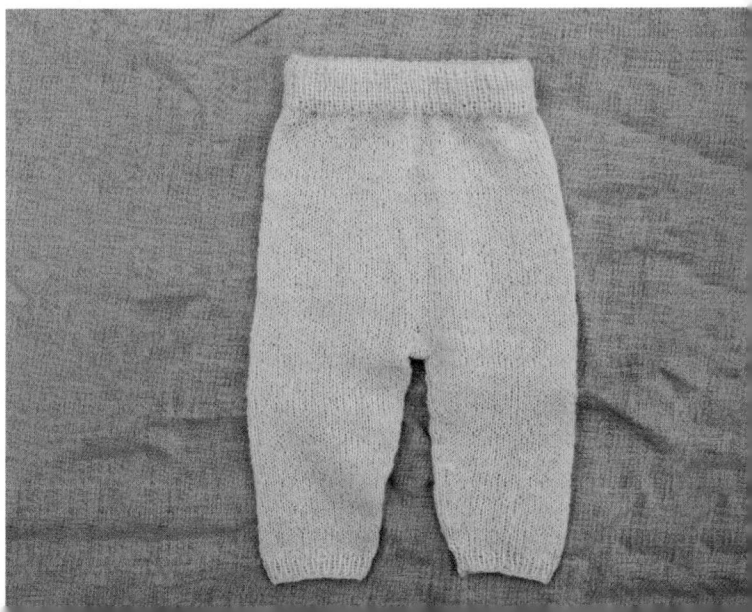

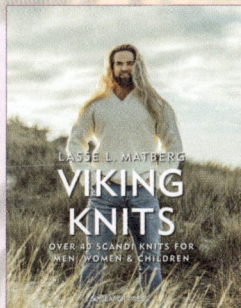

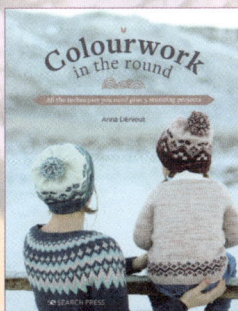

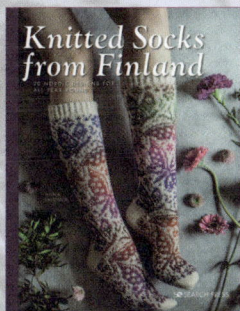

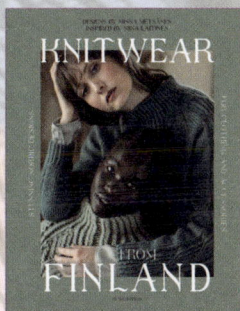

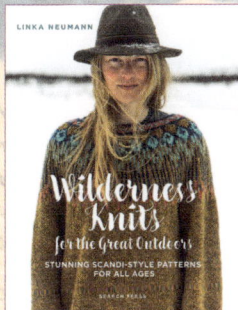

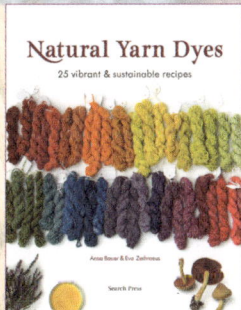

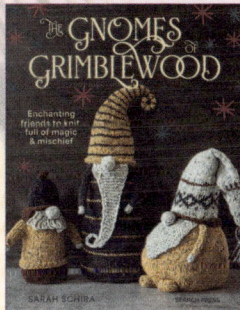